the MINDFULNESS *effect*

AN UNEXPECTED PATH TO HEALING, CONNECTION, & SOCIAL JUSTICE

DENA SAMUELS, PhD

NIGHT
RIVER
PRESS

The Mindfulness Effect: An unexpected journey to healing, connection, and social justice.

ISBN (Paperback): 978-1-7324836-0-6
ISBN (eBook): 978-1-7324836-1-3
ISBN (Audio Book): 978-1-7324836-2-0

Library of Congress Control Number: 2018949101

Front cover image: Dena Samuels PhD
Book & cover design: Matthew LaFleur

First printing edition 2018.

Samuels, Dena
    The mindfulness effect: an unexpected journey to healing, connection, and social justice / Dena Samuels
    p. cm.

Publisher Night River Press
Denver, CO, 80209
www.nightriverpress.com

Other books by author:
The Culturally Inclusive Educator: Preparing for a Multicultural World
(Teachers College Press, 2014)
The Matrix Reader: Examining the Dynamics of Oppression and Privilege
(McGraw-Hill, 2009)

Dedication

My Brilliant Image
One day the sun admitted, I am just a shadow. I wish I could show you the
Infinite Incandescence that has cast my brilliant image! I wish I could show you,
when you are lonely or in darkness, the Astonishing Light of your own Being
~ Hafiz

I dedicate this book to my openhearted and dearest friend, Daryl L. Miller, whose love and astonishing light will live on in my heart always.

Praise for *The Mindfulness Effect*

"Dr. Dena Samuels teaches with radical authenticity, courageous vulnerability, and deep wisdom. The Mindfulness Effect is a rich and practical manual for personal and collective healing, empowerment, and profound social justice."
~ **RABBI JESSICA KESSLER MARSHALL**

"*The Mindfulness Effect* has changed how I interact with the world and myself. I love how immediate and interactive it is! I've been unsure how to meditate in the past, I felt like I wasn't doing it right. I had no idea that meditation/mindfulness was so useful in self-healing. The practices really pulled me in and I ended up writing a meditation journal which was a useful tool of introspection. I see so much more clearly how mindfulness can help me lead a happy and more meaningful life. A life that I'm choosing. Also, the way the book seamlessly connected mindfulness and social justice changed my whole schematic. I wouldn't have thought of the connection before, but now I don't know how we would even try to resolve social justice issues without mindfulness and self-healing. Teaching people mindfulness helps them see their own biases and can soften their views on those who are different than themselves."
~ **JAIME PEDERSON, physical therapist**

"So much wisdom and caring is felt in these words and the simplicity with which the information about mindfulness is related is easy and inspiring to receive. Samuels' storytelling is an integral part of diving into the material, as it demonstrates the ideas and concepts in experiential form. As a kinetic learner, that helps me a lot. It also brings a rich creative hand to the book, moving it from instructional to "felt." … Samuels brings a most heart-satisfying, wholeness and healing gift to the world"
~ **NORMA JOHNSON, social justice poet & performing artist**

"So much to absorb and ponder. Thank you for this wonderful book! It's such a wise and also humble offering."
~ **DEBBIE ZUCKER, anti-racial activist and educator**

"This beautifully written and insightful book helps me understand more and more clearly that through mindfulness, meditation and decluttering practices, I am happier, healthier, more connected, more awake and conscious and aware. The practices Dr. Samuels encourages her readers to engage with are a journey toward personal freedom that also enables me/us to be of better service for social and environmental justice work." ~ **KRISTEN SUTTLES, writer**

Table of Contents

Acknowledgements/Pledge

This work has emerged from the inspiration and guidance of many friends and colleagues, based on the principle that defines it: a collaborative effort that is not fixed for all time, but rather dynamic, fluid, ever growing. This work is not mine, nor does it belong to me; it integrates the teachings of many scholars, yogis, and activists, many of whom are named in the book. As they have shared their teachings with me orally or in written form, I pledge to honor their wisdom and their example by continuing to teach these concepts and practices in service to others.

Students in my Social Justice & Sustainability: Living Mindfully course in the fall of 2015 served as the impetus and motivation to write this book. And it was Polly Fiedler, Kristen Suttles, Susan Patkin, Daryl Miller, Jenny Adams, among others who have guided and supported me in the process. I consider them my teachers, and for whom I have the utmost gratitude and respect.

For the inspiring conversations that informed this book, I thank: John Barber, Jaime Pedersen, Corinne Harmon, Mona Adelgren, Melinda Zolowicz, Sirat Salim, Stephany Rose, Shakti Butler, Steve Samuels, and Debby Irving; their enthusiastic words of encouragement have meant the world to me.

I offer gratitude also to those who have gently guided me to see the ways oppressive ideologies that exist in society have manifested within me. They have made visible what I was socialized not to see, so that I could mindfully do the work necessary to acknowledge, feel, mourn, and continue to release those ideologies from within that no longer serve me or the world. I thank in particular: Norma Johnson, Kenny Wiley, Todd Berliner, Heather Hackman, Alex Samuels, Harold Fields, Eddie Moore, Jr., Janice Gould, and Jessica Havens.

Thanks also to Kathy Sparrow for her detailed editing and insight; and to Skeeter Buck and Matthew LaFleur for their guidance and creativity. Finally, I offer gratitude to my daughter, Rachel Samuels, for her painstaking attention to my first draft. She offered a keen editorial eye, loving (and sometimes laugh-out-loud funny) feedback, and challenged me in ways that have transformed this book. I am inspired by her strength and determination to make this world a better, safer, more inclusive place for all of us, especially for those who have been silenced for too long.

Preface:
Cultivating Freedom from Within

*May the feeling of freedom you cultivate be so powerful
that others feel free when they are in your presence.*

You know that feeling you get when you're on vacation? When all your anxiety seems to dissipate and you can just be in the present moment, enjoying whatever experience comes along? Your vacation doesn't have to be a trip somewhere; sometimes it can happen in your own backyard, or in the next town over, or in visiting a park, or going for a hike or a bike ride, if that is available to you. When you get back home, you feel like you've been somewhere and you have a whole new perspective on your life. That feeling of freedom – that is the benefit of mindfulness. It is accessible any minute you choose throughout your day. And it doesn't cost a penny!

Mindfulness is an experience that in the midst of a busy day and a busy life, allows you to pause and focus on the present moment. It is an experience that is more easily understood through practice than words, and so this book provides 25 practices to get you started or move you forward on your journey toward freedom, peace, self-empowerment, culturally inclusive leadership, social justice, and environmental justice. In short, this book offers liberation: to achieve freedom through mindfulness practices. Mindfully connecting to your inner wisdom promotes: self-healing, belonging, and empowers you to discover your life's purpose and live a meaningful life. Mindfully connecting with others decreases unconscious bias, and promotes cultural inclusion and social justice. And mindfully connecting with the earth promotes environmental justice.

Let's meet on the leading edge: Are you ready to take your life, your organization, and the world, to the next level?

MY JOURNEY: FROM BREAKING DOWN TO BREAKING FREE

I have not always had a mindfulness practice. My background is in sociology and educational leadership. My career has been focused on cultural inclusion and social justice, and teaching about the importance of freedom from systemic oppression (racism, sexism, heterosexism, ableism, ageism, among others). Through my own harrowing journey from hell to healing, I realized the importance of personal freedom, and how to acquire it. My mindfulness practices provided a sense of serenity I had never before known or experienced.

Although this book is not a memoir, I share my experience here to provide a sense of how I have come to live a life of freedom from within. I had no idea when I was going through my journey, the impact mindfulness practices would have on my life, and how they connect perfectly with and enhance cultural inclusion and social justice practices. Every time I share my story, listeners seem to gain a better understanding of the tangible benefits of an effective mindfulness practice; they become curious to see how it might benefit their own lives.

Looking back on my life, I can't remember a time when I felt free. My first memories as a child are of being told to look pretty for the camera; already being forced to conform to the female standards of society. Standing on a large rock in the backyard of our house, I had on a yellow dress with a white bodice, little white socks, and patent-leather shoes, and I remember feeling like I had better measure up to whatever image my father, the photographer, had of what I was supposed to look like. I mustered a little grin on my face, stretched my dress out to the sides with my hands as if I were about to curtsy, and he snapped the photograph. Apparently, I passed the test. I was just four years old.

Despite the societal pressures of femininity that were already weighing down on my tiny body, that photograph stands out as being reminiscent of a relatively happy time. Unfortunately, it was extremely short-lived. My childhood home was not a safe place. I was subjected to severe trauma and every form of abuse (emotional, physical, and sexual), which trapped me in a continuous state of detachment, disconnection from my body, and disorientation. After my parents' divorce, my mother, with whom I lived, was incapacitated for two years. Fear and anxiety were my constant companions. And as our household wealth dwindled, I worried constantly that I wouldn't have light, heat, or food. I developed Obsessive-Compulsive Disorder as a coping strategy (needing to repeat behaviors an even number of times, as just one of so many symptoms), which I hid from everyone because I didn't want anyone to think something was wrong with me.

The only place I felt somewhat free was at school, where, fortunately, I excelled. I worked hard, sought out and received positive attention from my teachers, which motivated me to work even harder. Mercifully, throughout my adolescence and young adulthood, my clever brain blocked out much of my childhood torture and trauma as a means of self-protection. I had developed excellent strategies to erase any bad memories from my mind. My very effective coping techniques mostly centered on striving to be the best at everything I did. This strategy served me well in terms of meeting and exceeding the standards society sets for us.

Excelling meant I did not have time to stop and think, or feel. Thus, my time in college was jam-packed with activity: in addition to a full course load, I directed the entire dance program which included coordinating and teaching dance classes, and directing the largescale dance productions held on campus twice a year. In addition, I held three jobs to pay for college, and even made the dean's list. No downtime; no pauses in my over-filled days.

I met and eventually married Steve, a brilliant, grounded man from a two-parent, fairly normal, financially comfortable household, and we lived a very happy life for the next twenty years. It felt like a dream come true; I was living the life I had worked so hard to obtain. I was constantly moving at ˙warp-speed because for me that felt like happiness. Stopping to feel what my body was shielding me from was not an option.

Throughout that time, I managed to keep the nightmares I consistently experienced at bay. When my stress would overwhelm me, the nightmares would get worse, and made me terrified to go to sleep. They were so disturbing that once in my twenties and once in my thirties, I deliberately sought out short-term therapy in the hopes of relieving them. I just wanted them to go away, and although I did some important self-work both times, and learned some very important coping skills, I only went as deep as my conscience would allow at the time. I even hid my obsessive-compulsive tendencies from both counselors – and my husband – out of embarrassment for my behavior.

Instead, I continued to live at warp-speed, using my newly acquired coping skills when needed. By the time I was forty-five, I "had it all." I was the mother of two phenomenal children, whose classrooms I volunteered in every year; I was a faculty member at the university, had many good friends, and a loving relationship with my husband. I also volunteered as a conference coordinator for a national social justice conference, and was on the board of directors of my synagogue. I even had a freshly minted doctoral degree that I had completed in three years. Every day was a whirlwind of prioritization, coordination, and list-checking. In the United States, this is what "success" looks like.

And suddenly – unexpectedly – it all came crashing down.

With the challenging work of the doctoral program recently behind me, my brain was finally free to take a break. It wasn't long before my nightmares got so bad that the thought of getting into bed filled me with dread. My OCD-tendencies began to escalate, and my healthy coping strategies were no longer sufficient. I was exhausted from lack of sleep, and I felt triggered by too many of the things Steve unknowingly said or did. It became abundantly clear to me: It was time to return to therapy.

Since I did not understand why I was triggered by so many of Steve's actions and behaviors, I figured it was a marital problem. I was in such denial of my own suffering that I actually sought out a marriage counselor, and a male one, specifically with the hopes that Steve might be more comfortable with him. After sharing some of my history with the counselor who I thought would be our new therapist, the counselor gently suggested that he and I work together for a while, first.

It was time to unpack the nightmares. Suffice it to say I quickly discovered the nightmares I had suffered from for so many years were not dreams, but rather childhood memories of severe prolonged abuse both from family members and family friends. At one point, I remember my therapist giving me a book on survivors of incest. In spite of all the examples of it that I had already shared with him, the abhorrent behavior had been so normalized in my household that I never perceived it as incest. I looked at him, dumbfounded, saying, "Why are you giving me this? What's this got to do with me?" He simply paused, and calmly recommended I take the book home.

I reluctantly did so, carefully hiding it so neither Steve nor my children would find it and ask questions I couldn't answer. But it beckoned from underneath the stacks of paper I had put atop it, and so, several days later, I found the courage to open it. I was stunned that in the first pages there were lists of behaviors that fell under the category of childhood sexual abuse, and the tears streamed down my face as incredulously, I found I could check off every one.

That first year of therapy was filled with the pain of acknowledgement. Yes, this is in fact what happened to me. I could no longer ignore or even minimize it. The nightmares were real. And it was my experience. Just digesting that alone almost broke me.

Throughout that time, Steve was a rock for me. I cannot imagine how hard it must have been for him to see me shaking uncontrollably every night; my body trying to release the trauma it held. My biggest fear through it all was the impact my suffering would have on my children, so I tried, desperately, to hide it all from them. I can remember once my daughter walked into the bathroom where I was on the floor sobbing, trying not to vomit, gasping for air, remembering one of many torturous episodes of abuse. Steve was sitting next to me, serving as an anchor for me, seeing me through it. Even in my stupor, I was horrified that my daughter had witnessed this display of what I perceived at the time as weakness. I knew she always thought of me as strong, and strong meant capable; able to do everything, every day no matter what, and as perfectly as possible. That's what I strove to teach her. That was the message I had wanted her to receive. This was not that.

The next few years brought about more internal pain and suffering. Through it all, I did the best I could to provide as much stability in the home as I could. I took everything else off my plate aside from my kids, my part-time job teaching about sexism and racism at the university (no small feat during this time), and healing myself. As suicidal as I might have been when I woke up each morning, unable to decipher between my perpetual nightmares/memories and my current reality, by 3:00 when the kids got home from school every day, I made sure, at the very least, to have gotten up and showered to welcome them home.

Many Indigenous and First Nations communities tend to practice restorative justice for healing from personal harm inflicted by another/ others; however, in westernized society, we are taught to blame. Some of my close friends wanted to blame my perpetrators for the pain they had caused me. And it was a healthy step for me to take along my healing journey. And when the time came to forgive, I did so for my own health and well-being. I no longer wanted to carry around the anger and hurt that I was feeling toward my perpetrators. It took me several years of deep inner-work and healing, but I was finally able to forgive – not for them, but for me. "Forgiving" is "giving-for" me. It is for my benefit; no one else's.

At this point, the reasons for my experience are continually unfolding to me, and I am confident that the situation that caused my pain showed up specifically for me in the service of my own growth and learning, and perhaps in service to others as I share my experience. I love the saying, "Life doesn't happen *to* us; it happens *for* us." Even if we can't see the big picture at the time, sometimes we get a glimpse later of what we perceive to be the real purpose of experiencing what we had to go through to get where we are.

I do not believe I would have made it through the Post-Traumatic Stress I endured without the help of therapy, my devoted husband (a close friend now), a few of my nearest and dearest friends, my kids who gave me hope and a reason to stick around, the teachings of yoga, and a newly acquired mindfulness practice. Although I was raised secularly Jewish, at this point in my life, I was much more drawn to eastern and Indigenous philosophies, and Buddhist practices. I began to study deeply about the nature of our existence, and what/who we really are that goes beyond the bodies we inhabit. I began to understand that we are spiritual beings in physical bodies as opposed to physical beings who sometimes have a spiritual experience.

As I began to see myself differently, I began to see the world differently, and I could finally envision a way out of all (or at least most) of the suffering. With all of the guidance I received from my support team as well as the studying I was engaged in, I was able to let go of the unhealthy coping strategies I had utilized my whole life: never slowing down, OCD, among others. I emerged a few years later, healthier and more peaceful than I have ever been in my whole life. Scholar and author Dr. Brené Brown aptly refers to her own "breakdown" as a spiritual breakthrough. This fits my own experience perfectly.

I learned that in order to live healthy lives, inside and out, we must recognize the sacredness in ourselves. If we can see ourselves as part of the greater Universe, as holy beings, it is less likely we will harm ourselves or treat ourselves poorly or in unhealthy ways. This does not have to be a religious perspective at all, though it can be. It is not religious for me, though I respect it if it is for you. It doesn't even have to be a spiritual idea, even though it is for me. It can simply be the idea that we are much more than the sum of our parts. In other words, who/what we really are, is more than the emotions we are having, or the bodies we inhabit, or our judgments about those bodies. Yes, those are facets of what we might experience on a daily basis in the physical world, but it is not the sum total of who/what we are.

These notions of how we perceive ourselves will be covered in much greater detail later, but for now, consider it this way: If we reduce ourselves to the fear we feel, or the shame we experience, or the number on the scale, or the boss' feedback, we are missing out on the rest of our life's experience. We get completely immersed in the emotional or physical pain we are suffering through, and cannot see beyond it. On the other hand, conscious awareness of our full expansiveness at any given moment (one of the mindfulness practices that will be described in this book) is the antidote to human physical or emotional suffering. It's that simple.

My foray into mindfulness practices started with a daily meditation in the morning. I used a meditation app on my phone, which I found to be quite useful. I could set the length of time I wanted to meditate and also found that there were so many guided meditations which helped me to get quiet, be still, and focus on my breathing for a while. In the beginning, I was motivated by the fact that the app tracked my daily practice, so I felt compelled to see how many days of meditation I could achieve in a row. Although my practice has since shifted away from grasping for an attachment to the outcome, the app helped me develop, and even get excited about, a consistent practice.

Through studying about meditation and mindfulness practices, I learned that many teachers (especially those in the Zen tradition) insist on sitting up when one is meditating. I found I was much less likely to get out of a warm bed to meditate, however, so I began to meditate lying down in my cozy bed. Some would say it is problematic that I would sometimes fall asleep. I never saw it that way, though. I always figured if I fell asleep, then my body needed sleep more than the meditation. Additionally, it was a very peaceful sleep, which was a welcome change for me! When I awoke, I would simply start my meditation again, even if I was left only with a few moments before I had to get out of bed and start my day.

Within a few months, I noticed the effect that mindfulness meditation was having on my life. I started to notice my breath throughout the day, not just during my meditations. If I was focusing on my breath, it usually meant I was pausing in a potentially stressful situation before responding, as opposed to immediately, and often irrationally, reacting. This increased the likelihood of peaceful solutions rather than an escalation of tension. This made driving in traffic a reflective time instead of a stressful time. And because I meditated in the morning when I first woke up, I was able to clear my head of any lingering horror from my nightmares, feel any emotions that were arising, let them go, and set an intention for the day ahead.

When I first started setting an intention, it was often as simple as to stay grounded as often as possible that day. This is what I needed during that time. As I began to heal, and discover who/what I really am, my intention was to remember who/what I really am as often as possible throughout my day. More recently, my intention has transformed to become both inward and outward-focused. It is to connect to my expanded awareness as often as possible throughout the day, and to seek out opportunities to be of service to others.

In addition to clarifying my life's purpose, and healing from trauma, my mindfulness practices also allowed me to reframe my lived experience: what I considered to be reality and what I considered illusion. During the time of dealing with my trauma, I lived in the illusion of my past story as though it were still happening; as though I were still in danger for my life. Closing my eyes used to bring up my trauma and horrible memories; fear and terror would rise in me to the point that I was frightened to go to sleep. As I began to heal from Post-Traumatic Stress, I found comfort, solidity, and deep gratitude when I opened my eyes. The four walls and ceiling were grounding for me – a reality I could grasp that assured me that I was here now in this moment and no longer trapped in the terror of my past.

It has been a long journey, but I am proud to say that now when I close my eyes, I find that in place of terror is serenity. I immediately remember my expansive sacredness. I have learned to connect to who I really am. This is my reality. This is where I find everlasting peace and unlimited possibility. This is my resource: where I re-source myself, finding invigorating energy and intention.

And the incredible thing is, mindfulness practices now allow me to feel and be connected to who I really am even when my eyes are open. Even when I'm in the midst of a conversation with someone, my practices serve to make my words authentic. They sharpen my listening skills and free me to live in and put forth peaceful, healing energy into the world and toward those around me.

Through my practices, I began to uncover my life's purpose. I had known for a long time that I was called to teach, for it has always been in the classroom, connecting with students that I have felt most useful and most of service. Over time, it was more than just in the classroom that I noticed feeling in alignment with my spiritual calling; I feel it now whenever I am connecting with others, on a call from a friend or family member in need, facilitating a keynote or workshop, teaching a yoga class, or offering personal or professional coaching. My ego dissolves, and love, peace, and the encouragement of infinite possibility flows out of me.

Over time, I was finally able to acknowledge and verbalize my life's intention/passion/purpose: To be of service to others by elevating consciousness and supporting people in their search for internal empowerment so they can live intentional, liberated, healthy lives, and engage in authentic, deeply meaningful relationships, especially across social differences.

More succinctly stated: my intention is to alleviate suffering by: elevating spiritual consciousness (guiding people on their journey toward becoming awakened) and elevating social consciousness (guiding people on their journey toward becoming "woke").

I do not profess to be awakened or woke because both are lifelong journeys, but I have dedicated my life to both of these paths, and have watched them intersect. Hence, this book was born in the hope of providing a path for you to tap into your own healing, empowerment, vision; in short, to live a more meaningful life, and to connect deeply and authentically with others.

This book offers some of the ways I have found to use mindfulness practices to transform my daily lived experience into a healthy, joyful, abundant life in which I am aligned with my highest purpose and a true sense of meaning. If we consider ourselves as holy, sacred, valuable (insert the word here that resonates with you and throw out the rest) beings, we will treat ourselves as such. This has substantial consequences for our personal health and well-being.

Moreover, as we use mindfulness practices to connect with/get to know, understand, and appreciate people whose social identities (race, gender, sexuality, age, physical or mental capacity, etc.) are different from our own, we begin to increase our compassion. And if we consider others as holy, sacred, valuable (again, insert the word that resonates with you and throw out the rest) beings, we will treat them as such. This has substantial consequences for cultural inclusion and social justice. It is harder to ignore injustice or the mistreatment of others if we see them as precious beings connected to our lives, right?

Finally, we can use mindfulness practices to heal the planet. For if we consider the Earth as cherished or sacred, it is difficult to hurt it. More so, if we mindfully connect with the Earth, we can promote healing for it and all of its inhabitants for generations to come.

The title of this book is purposefully reminiscent of the concept known as "the butterfly effect." In 1992, chaos theorist Edward Lorenz coined the term to describe the potential impact of the minor flap of a butterfly's wings in one part of the world on the weather patterns in another part of the world. Although difficult to predict, even minor actions can have serious consequences. If we each engage in mindful behavior as often as possible, consider the tremendous effect we could have on the planet.

Introduction:
What is Mindful Liberation?

In this moment, there is plenty of time. In this moment, you are precisely as you should be. In this moment, there is infinite possibility.
~Victoria Moran

I was at my dear friend Norma's house recently. Over a potful of scrumptious oatmeal that she was lovingly cooking for us, we were engaging in a conversation about life, our place in it, and our connection to current political and environmental events. She made a profound statement that stuck with me. She said, "We're on the precipice of a new frontier. We need something more. We're all looking for a new answer; a new way of thinking, of being. It's time to evolve."

We are in need of both individual and collective liberation from the social and systemic ties that bind us. We need to feel empowered in ourselves, and gain a sense of belonging that allows us to explore and expand our innate and powerful creativity that can move mountains, and solve the world's inequities. Mindfulness offers a sense of personal and collective freedom.

Mindfulness practices have allowed me to experience and understand my place in the world. They have allowed me to discover my home within. While I am on this planet, I choose to:
- live my life as fully and with as much meaning as I possibly can;
- fulfill my life's purpose, and to be in alignment with that purpose each day;
- challenge systems of inequality that provide access and a feeling of inclusion to some and not to others;
- build authentic relationships across cultural differences to cultivate a sense of connection and belonging; and
- develop the symbiotic relationship we all have with the planet as a social justice imperative for the health and wellbeing of myself and all of the earth's inhabitants.

I have found that mindfulness is a means for achieving all of these goals. What might it do for you?

In my twenty years as a sociologist, researcher, college professor, and national diversity and inclusion speaker and consultant, I have always focused on self-reflection and personal transformation. As my journey progressed to include mindfulness practices that increased my own health and wellbeing, I also began to see the ways in which this tool could be used for healing our relationships with each other, and with the planet. It seemed like a perfect extension of my yogic philosophy and practice, and a prescription for cultural exclusion, as well as social and environmental injustice. The more I learned, the more I was compelled and excited to share these ideas and practices.

Given the state of our current socio-political climate, we do, in fact, need a major shift in what we know to be our reality. The mindfulness practices provided in this book serve to alleviate at least some of the suffering we all experience, perhaps in different ways, but all as human beings. My passion revolves around the notion that mindfulness can be used as a tool for personal healing, self-empowerment, culturally inclusive leadership, equity, and environmental justice, and once familiar with the practices, is accessible to everyone at any moment. All it takes is the practice of remembering that this tool exists, and implementing it.

A local community activist shared with me recently that when he speaks to community members, his deep theoretical analysis of structural inequities is often met with the rejoinder, "These are powerful ideas, but how are we gonna' feed the babies?" Participants in his talks are usually dealing with the daily struggle of those inequities, and this question gets to the heart of that struggle. I appreciate the question and have attempted to keep it in my mind as I share some theory and practices of mindfulness in this book. I am not suggesting that mindfulness practices are a panacea to heal all suffering; rather, they are a readily-accessible tool that can be used to make visible and challenge those unfair systems that have very real consequences.

The benefits of mindfulness have been touted by many. The fields of neurology, psychology, health/medicine, and many others agree on the plethora of medical benefits of mindfulness. It can change our brain chemistry and calm our parasympathetic system which means less stress, an increased sense of peace, improved health and wellbeing, and the list goes on. These studies have gone a long way in making mindfulness more widely valued and accessible, so that mindfulness is now taught in schools, universities, prisons, and many leading-edge, financially successful corporations that have a commitment to conscious business practices.

The research that struck me the most, however, was scholars Lueke and

Gibson's article in 2014, "Mindfulness Meditation Reduces Implicit Age and Race Bias." When I read this, my worlds collided! I had been teaching implicit bias trainings/workshops for years, and separately, I taught mindfulness as a means of healing and self-empowerment. The scientific community was beginning to connect the dots, and immediately the focus of my work began to change. Specifically, I began to incorporate mindfulness practices in my anti-bias trainings as strategies for more effective interactions, and for building deeper relationships across social differences. Moreover, I found these practices can be used to both notice and challenge systems of inequity, in other words, as a tool for social justice. I offer these and many other practices in this book.

A simple internet search will demonstrate that more and more corporations, institutions, and organizations are making use of mindfulness, yet these practices are not new. Mindfulness is rooted in Ancient Eastern teachings. My understanding is that mindfulness practices are to be shared for the purpose of peace within and without. I have only put these ideas into a format and in words, images, activities and practices that I hope you will find accessible and useful, with the deepest respect for my forbears – those who have been offering these kinds of teachings for centuries.

Even though Eastern and Indigenous cultures teach that the concepts of healing, and social and environmental justice are intertwined, overwhelmingly, the westernized world is only beginning to embrace this kind of thinking. (And by westernized world, I am not referring to the geographic region, for we live on colonized Indigenous land, but rather to what is currently considered Eurocentric, or mainstream, culture.) The way I explain the connection between mindfulness and these other concepts is like this: Mindfulness practices help us to slow down and pay attention. Taking the time to notice our thoughts and behaviors allows us to choose to act and interact differently. This has implications for our own wellbeing, and our connections with others, and with the planet.

Because we now live in an increasingly segregated society, we are not building relationships across differences. Instead, on the rare occasion that we interact with someone whose social identities are different than our own, be it a different race, sexual orientation, etc., we tend to rely on misinformation and overused stereotypes, which gives us the illusion that we know them. We tend to react based on those stereotypes, rather than to respond mindfully, and the contact tends to be superficial. Mindfulness practices allow us to notice our own biases so we can form deeper, more meaningful relationships across race, gender, sexuality, social class, disability, among other social identities, expanding our life and experiences beyond what anyone could imagine was possible.

As I explained in my last book, *The Culturally Inclusive Educator: Preparing for a Multicultural World*, we in the United States, are not prepared to build cultural inclusiveness, even though we think we are. My national research showed that, regardless of race, those who were more likely to think they were culturally inclusive were less likely to actually engage in the best inclusive practices that were culled from the top research and scholars in the field at the time. Best practices included engaging in meaningful dialogue around issues of diversity and inclusion, including the historical legacy of systemic discrimination, incorporating several social identities into analyses and discussions (race, gender, sexuality, social class, etc.), bringing diverse perspectives into the conversations on these topics, among others.

The research showed that those who felt they were and should be "color-blind" or post-racialist – treating everyone the same, the less likely they were to be culturally inclusive. We have little to no meaningful education in engaging in culturally inclusive practices and because of segregation, have little to no contact across differences. Because of this, we are ill-prepared to build cultural inclusion. We want to believe because we are "good people" and we treat everyone with respect that that will be enough to create cultural inclusion. Turns out, it's not enough.

That research highlights the fact that we need strategies and techniques for learning to be inclusive. This book will provide mindfulness practices that are designed to take our social contexts into account, as opposed to ignoring our social identities – a tendency that occurs in many spiritual enclaves (more about this later). With some guidance, we can use mindfulness practices to minimize our unintentional biases, and learn to authentically engage with others across social differences in order to form deep, meaningful relationships. In addition, the more we embrace those differences and mindfully consider our own social identities, the more likely we will be to see, acknowledge, and challenge the systems of social inequities that exist, to work toward creating a more socially just world.

We are in the midst of a substantial ideological, polarizing cultural clash that becomes more pronounced as time goes on. Fear is being sold cheaply, and many people are buying into it. The "us" vs. "them" mentality breeds fear: fear that we are not enough; that we don't have enough; that there is not enough. That the more others succeed, the more we are likely to fail. The more they get, the less we do. When fear abounds, segregation ensues. And when we isolate ourselves, we minimize our lives, our experiences, and our sense of belonging in the world. There is an alternative practice – we can look within.

WHAT IS MINDFULNESS?

At this point, I have asked hundreds, if not thousands of students and workshop participants to define mindfulness. I often hear the same words to describe it: focusing on the present moment, awareness, awakening, conscious, present, alert, open, attentive, letting go, non-judgment, non-attachment. It can be described as the experience of fully connecting with the present moment, where everything slows down and there is a sense of peace and wholeness about you. Where you let go of the events of the day or the situation you currently find yourself in, and pay attention to this moment. Ultimately, it is something that is more easily experienced than described.

One of my colleagues told me she gets very uncomfortable when she hears the word mindfulness. She says she thinks of it as praying, and doesn't like the religious connotation. She feels obliged to participate whether she wants to or not, and that doesn't feel good to her. I thanked her for sharing her trepidation with me because it reminds me to continually highlight the fact that mindfulness is not a religious practice. For some it can be, but for many people, including me, it is simply the practice of stepping into the present moment, for the present is all we truly have. The past we cannot change, and the future is subject to many things beyond our control. All we know for certain is what we are experiencing in this moment.

I like to begin defining mindfulness as a way of cultivating stillness in our busy lives. But it's more than focusing on our breath. The definition expands to include the philosophy of accepting what is, with compassion, and without judgment. We are so often taught, conditioned really, to judge ourselves and others harshly. Mindfulness provides a means of stepping back and allowing life to be just as it is and progress just as it does.

This does not mean that we should allow injustices to exist. Rather it means we are less focused on the outcome of an argument that centers on who is right and who is wrong. Mindfulness provides space in our lives, and allows us to pause and respond, rather than react. Victor E. Frankl's words sums this up best:

"Between stimulus and response there is a space. In that space is our power to choose our response. In our response lies our growth and our freedom."

Many Indigenous cultures teach us to connect our shared past with a shared future. Known as the 7th Generation principle, and codified in the Iroquois Great Law of Peace, it is suggested that with every decision we make, we must consider and show gratitude to the ancestors who came before us, and to take into account seven generations into the future. In so doing, we acquire a much broader perspective. Mindfulness provides a path toward inner peace and joy through an expanded connection to all living beings, which also results in an enhanced sense of belonging.

Many mindfulness practices exist. A few of these are: traditional meditation, informal meditation, mindful walking, mindful eating, focusing on the breath and/or senses, mindful pausing, metta or lovingkindness meditation. This book will touch on some of these and more, in the form of meditation practices in every chapter. This introduction provides a few to get started. Before we practice, however, consider these ideas about this book:

- If you are reading this book, it likely means you are already on your path to live your best life; you already possess an Inner Knowing about how to do that; with mindfulness practices, this book serves only to offer you direction for deeply listening to, and being guided by, that Inner Knowing.

- As is true for most learning and/or developing, mindfulness takes a commitment to consistent practice as opposed to once in a while. As you begin (or continue) to experience its benefits, it is likely that you will want to practice more. To get the most out of this book and these practices, I recommend showing up with a willingness to engage in deep self-reflection of mind, body, and spirit.

- Spirituality as expressed in this book means finding deep meaning and purpose in your life and connecting with something greater than the body you inhabit. If there is a connection between spirituality and religion for you, feel free to view it that way, or not; the choice is yours.

- I approach this book from an intersectional perspective, meaning that we all have social identities that impact our lives and experiences. We all have a race, a gender, a sexuality, a social class, etc., and we will reflect on how those identities operate in our lives, and influence our interactions with others. When I use the term "we" in this book, I am referring to our shared sense of what it means to be human. At the same time, the skin we are in matters. Thus, I approach this work with a deep recognition and understanding that I am coming from a white, cisgender female, bisexual, middle-class, non-disabled lens, and that those identities influence how I see the world.

- There are many practices and activities in this book, and they build on each other. I suggest engaging with them in the order in which they were written since there is a purposeful progression. That said, this is your journey, so feel free to take it at your own pace and in your own way. Make it your own!

Finally, the premise of the book revolves around the need our society has both for spiritual awakening and for an awakened/woke social consciousness. This book attempts to raise our awareness and skill-level in both, not with an endpoint in mind, but rather as a lifelong process.

MINDFULNESS MEDITATION

I hear many people say they are "bad" at meditation. But truly there is no such thing as being bad at it because it is a practice. As one of my clients recently pointed out, "It's time to let go of the story I've been telling myself that I am a bad meditator. It's not helpful and keeps me from the possibility of learning how to do it!"

In his audiobook, *Spontaneous Awakening*, Adyashanti describes meditation as an opportunity to stop searching for answers or manipulating our thoughts, rather just being; letting go. I hope to provide some direction of how to allow that process to happen.

When starting out, the process of mindfulness meditation might go something like this:

1. Focus on your breath (your inhales and exhales);
2. When (not if) you notice you've begun to follow the thought(s) that inevitably arise, come back to your breath;
3. Repeat #1 and #2 over and over for whatever period of time you've chosen to practice.

That's the basic practice, although this book will offer other versions that will go much deeper. Most people who say they're "bad" at it think they've done something wrong if they tried to focus on their breath and got caught up in one or more of their thoughts and then forgot all about focusing on their breath. This is not a problem; this is what we do as human beings! The practice is to realize your mind has gone astray and then to return to focusing on the breath. Starting out, it may take several minutes or more of thinking thoughts before you realize you've gotten caught in your thoughts. As you progress, it takes less and less time for you to remember, and you come back to your breath in a shorter amount of time. This book provides many different mindfulness meditations, but steps 1-3 above constitute the basic practice and are a good place to start. Even for five minutes a day. See for yourself the impact it can have on your life.

Keep in mind, too, that mindfulness meditation is not a destination, but rather a journey. There is no need to do it perfectly; you don't get an "A" for effort. It is simply a practice with no attachment to the outcome of it.

When I first started meditating, I didn't love it. I did it because I had heard the positive effects it could have, and I thought it was worth trying. It wasn't long before I did notice its impact and life-changing potential. It took a few years of daily practice, however, before I really began to look forward to it. Now, I truly love how it feels to get lost in what I like to call the space between thoughts.

I appreciate spiritual leader and author, Eckhart Tolle's critique of the word *mindfulness*. He suggests that it should really be called *mindlessness* since the practice allows us to de-clutter thinking mind and find some peaceful space. All earthly pressures and anxiety melt away, and I am free to connect with the Universe, ask questions and listen for answers from my Inner Knowing/Inner Guide, imagine myself as big or small as I want, sometimes as a bird soaring through the air. That freedom stays with me at the end of my meditation when I open my eyes. I carry that sense with me throughout the day, and even in my interactions with other people. And it often allows me to start my day with newfound intention or purpose based on the insights I gained during my meditation.

Whatever you hope to get from this book, I encourage you to approach it with the Zen Buddhist philosophy known as Beginner's Mind. Approaching situations with an "I know" mentality, as dominant culture teaches us to do, can end up disallowing the potential and opportunity for growth and learning. Beginner's Mind, on the other hand, encourages us to approach what we are learning from a place of "I don't know" – a place of curiosity. Even if there are aspects of this book that you think you know, using Beginner's Mind ensures you will learn no matter what your background and experience is with mindfulness practices and/or with social justice.

Let's get started!

MINDFULNESS PRACTICES

If you are new to mindfulness practices, I highly recommend beginning with the first two practices below. If you are more experienced, I still recommend beginning with these to get a feel for the format of this book, and in the spirit of Beginner's Mind. I suggest trying all the practices provided throughout the book at least once so you can have a toolkit full of practices by the time you finish the book. Some of the mindfulness practices may resonate more than others. You'll know the practice is a good fit if it speaks to you in some way. If there are practices that stand out to you, or leave you feeling moved, or motivated, or just plain good, add them to your repertoire and practice them again and again. This is how you build your practice.

Ideally, I would be providing these practices orally so that you could just close your eyes and focus on the exercise rather than having to read the words and experience the practice at the same time. If you have access, feel free to head to my website so you can download or stream each mindfulness practice. If you don't have access to the Internet, perhaps you can ask a friend to read them to you.

Each of the practices in this book are offered with the knowledge that most adults have come through some sort of adversity or trauma in their lives. You do not need to have suffered trauma to find the activities and practices useful, but given the daunting statistics on abuse and trauma, I have tried to be sensitive to the needs of survivors throughout. One of the many ways I do this is to acknowledge that for some trauma survivors, closing their eyes and focusing inward, or even focusing on their bodies can be an insurmountable challenge at times, depending on where they are in their healing process. I suggest the option of gazing down instead of closing your eyes if that applies to you, or if that feels better to you for any reason.

If any of the practices throughout the book bring up feelings that are overwhelming or too unpleasant, feel free to take a break, and return later. Feel free to seek out assistance from a friend, family member, counselor, or therapist. Ultimately, the goal is health and wellness for you, and for your relationships. Please proceed knowing and attending to your own personal needs.

Taking this idea further, keep in mind that our bodies can look and feel very different, one person to another. I have attempted to acknowledge these differences whenever possible, noting the phrase, "if it's available to you" which is common in adaptive yoga classes, and reminds us to be mindful of the fact that what is possible for one body may not be possible for another. My goal is to be as inclusive as I can be, knowing that I will likely miss the mark in places. I am and will forever be a lifelong learner, doing my best to incorporate what I learn as I go. In so doing, I hope to challenge the assumption that our bodies are or should be all the same, and instead, to embrace our differences. What I request of you is to proceed with compassion to yourself, your body, and to me if/when I miss the mark!

As you move through this book, each time you complete one of the mindfulness practices, I strongly urge you to spend a few moments writing about your experience in a journal or notebook. If you are new to these practices, you might be surprised to discover insights, and what arises in you from these meditations. It can be helpful to write these inspired insights down so you can refer back to them later – either to track your progress, or more importantly, to decide if you want to take action on what you've discovered about yourself. This is your mindfulness journey. Dare to engage and get the most out of it!

MINDFULNESS PRACTICE 1
Present Moment/Finding Stillness/Focusing on the Breath

Find a comfortable seat in a quiet space, sitting up if you can, but doing whatever feels comfortable to your body. If it's possible to sit in a chair with your feet on the floor, please do so. If that doesn't work for you or your body, feel free to be in whatever position works best for you. It is most important to find the position where you are least distracted, where you can focus. If it is available to you, feel free to close your eyes, if not, feel free to gaze down.

Take a deep breath in, and as you exhale, allow your body to settle into this moment. On your next full breath in, focus on all the things that are swirling around in your brain from your day, and as you exhale, see if you can let all or any of them, go. Let go of the past and the future to focus on your now. This may take a few rounds of deep breaths. Come into this moment more and more. Be aware of your body in your seat. Feel where your body connects with the chair. Feel where your body connects with the earth, even if you are up several stories in the building you are in.

If it's available to you, notice your breath. Notice where in your body you feel your breath coming in and out. Do you feel it in your chest as your chest rises and falls? Do you feel it in your belly as your belly expands and contracts? Do you feel it underneath your nostrils where the air heats up your upper lip as it is expelled from your lungs? Just notice. There is no right or wrong here. It's just what you are experiencing in this present moment. Continue to focus on your inhales and exhales.

If it is too uncomfortable for you to focus inwardly on your breath for whatever reason – due to trauma, or pain, or anything else that might be triggering for you, feel free to focus instead on the words on the page. Concentrate on the texture of the page, the blackness of the letters on the white page, etc. Or focus on the details of some object in front of you. You will get the same benefit from doing it this way. Whatever brings you into the present moment and allows you to find some inner stillness is what is important. Continue to breathe.

As your mind starts to wander, which our minds are prone to do, continue to bring it back to your breath, the words on the page, or the object in front of you. Again, and again, and again. This practice of continually refocusing is, in itself, one way to meditate. See if you can continue this practice for five minutes. When you are done, open your eyes if they were closed, stretch your body in whatever way it feels it needs to stretch. Take a moment to transition your focus back to your surroundings and notice how you feel.

Welcome back.

Feel free to journal now about your experience, or about any ideas or insights that arose for you.

This mindfulness practice is one you can use every day. A longer outbreath soothes the parasympathetic system and serves to calm us down. If you can find your pulse on your wrist or neck, then notice how the beating of your heart slows on the exhale. You can practice it for five minutes a day at a specific time, and/or use it to come back to the present moment throughout your day when you are feeling any kind of stress. I use it when I'm waiting in line at the store or sitting in traffic. It is a valuable tool to live a life of inner peace.

It can also be used as a starting place for any of the other mindfulness practices in this book. It can be a jumping off point. You could practice this for a few moments and when you are ready, add another practice to it.

Find a comfortable seat. Take a deep breath and come into this moment. As you exhale, let go of your day. Feel your body in your seat. Feel the energy of the earth coming up through whatever part of your body is closest to or touching the floor. As you breathe in, imagine the energy from the earth making its way up your body and up your spine, and then as you exhale, breathe the energy right out the crown of your head. Repeat this pattern several times.

When you are ready, settle into your seat. Notice your breathing pattern. Then, notice where your thoughts go. Is your mind filled with thoughts making lots of distracting chatter? Or are you having one thought at a time? Know that this is what minds do. They think thoughts.

Imagine you are sitting comfortably by a stream. Look around you and notice the trees and the earth beneath you. And then draw your attention to the stream in front of you. Notice the water gently streaming in one direction. And when your next distracting thought arises, see if you can imagine placing the thought, whatever it is, onto a leaf upstream. Look at the thought on the leaf. What emotion arises about the thought? Can you release any judgment of yourself for thinking the thought, and release any judgment you may have about the thought itself?

Now let the leaf go and watch it slowly meander downstream. And as it goes out of sight, wave it goodbye. And as soon as the next thought comes up, notice it. Place it on another leaf upstream, let go of all judgment, and watch it find its way slowly downstream and wave it goodbye. Continue this process for a minimum of five minutes.

Another variation you can try is to picture yourself in a very green field or on the beach looking up at a very blue sky. Each thought that arises can be placed on a fluffy white cloud in the sky. Let go of all judgment, and watch it slowly make its way across the sky and wave it goodbye. Repeat this process for as long as you've chosen to meditate.

When you're ready, take a deep breath, stretch your body and take a moment to transition your focus back into the room.

Welcome back.

Feel free to journal now about your experience, or about any ideas or insights that arose for you.

This practice helps you to notice that your thoughts are just thoughts. We humans have a lot of them throughout the day. As Dr. Deepak Chopra claims, "We have approximately 60,000 thoughts in a day. Unfortunately, 95% of them are thoughts we had the day before." Our thoughts can inspire us to take action, or they can bring about a whole lot of pain. We can choose to get caught up in them and allow them to take us on a journey; or we can recognize them for what they are: a thought, and let them go. We have a choice.

Using Beginner's Mind, in this book, we will delve into who/what we really are, how we want to show up, why we are here, how we have been taught to be and how to release some of those stale ideas to find meaning and purpose. Further, I offer mindfulness practices that can be used to heal and grow our relationships with others. Building authentic relationships, especially across social differences, is a key antidote to social injustice.

CHAPTER 1

Social Conditioning – Living from the Outside In

"Our limited perceptions get in the way of our greatness"
~Dr. Shakti Butler, World Trust

I used to wake up in the morning and reach for my cellphone. I would start off each day scrolling through the endless posts on Facebook, and I would be overcome with a sense of paralysis – unable to move because what I was reading was so devastatingly inconceivable: human catastrophes, political turmoil, the decimation of civil rights, climate impact on a global scale from over-industrialization, and many other earthly, human-made problems. Although awareness of these problems is an important responsibility, my rate of exposure to them was overwhelming.

The more I read, the more my stomach would churn, the more my shoulders would tighten, the more uncomfortable I would feel about life – not just life in general, but my own life. I would begin to feel unsafe, insecure, doubting myself and my future. I would be mired in uncertainty and a mentality of scarcity: that there simply is not enough in the world, and moreover, I am not enough. This is how I would start each day: living from the outside in, tossed around like a newborn duckling in a torrential rainstorm, feeling battered, beaten, helpless, and defenseless against the uncontrollable onslaught of life.

We are constantly bombarded by societal messages that perpetuate the notion that we have no control over anything – that the world is on a crash course to hell and there's no turning back. We are constantly told we are not enough and that we do not have enough. And that the only way to gain control over anything (or anyone) is to pay for it. Even a seemingly innocuous advertisement that shows a "before" and "after" picture sells the idea that we are not enough, and if we just buy this product, then we will be better – at least until we see the next ad trying to make us believe we still are not enough or still don't have enough. For the right price, we can buy anti-aging creams that will control the barrage of wrinkles from (the natural, healthy process of) aging, or control-top pantyhose for women that smooth anything that might shatter the illusion of a flat tummy, or a plethora of erection-sustaining pills so that men can take control over their sex lives. The message is clear: if we buy this product, we will be able to control our lives.

The more we are made to believe the world is chaotic, the more fearful we become, and the more we feel we need to control both our fear and the world. The antidote, or so we are told/sold, is to increase our economic power. Thus, we buy into, and consequently perpetuate, a system of greed and domination. We are so accustomed and conditioned to these ideas that they may not even register as being problematic. The ideology of "not enough" is embedded in us. It manifests within us because it is in the air we breathe. It has infected us like a virus and we do not even know we are sick, and the consequences are dire.

We are conditioned to hold up gluttony as the ideal: over-spending, overeating, overindulging. And it's a vicious cycle because once we overindulge, we then want to control our over-indulgences (the weight loss industry is a multi-billion-dollar industry, as just one example), until we are ready to overindulge the next time (most crash course weight-loss programs are ineffective in the long-term). And as the U.S. wealth gap continues to escalate, people who are already wealthy desperately chase the almighty dollar, and somehow remain overwhelmingly unfulfilled, while people in poverty increasingly cannot make ends meet. The argument is if we make more and spend more, then eventually we will be fulfilled.

Global social psychological researcher, Dr. Sonja Lyubomirsky, however, found that no matter where you live, once you have reached subsistence levels (that you can pay your basic bills each month without worry), an increase in income beyond that amount no longer correlates with an increase in happiness. In other words, there is no significant difference in happiness/satisfaction between a single person making $50,000 in the U.S. and a person making $50,000,000. Beyond subsistence-level, happiness can no longer be bought.

This happiness research provides a marked difference in what we have been conditioned to believe about making money. And it demonstrates how power and privilege have been leveraged against the average hard-working individual.

Who wins when people work even harder for their money, and ultimately spend more of what they earn because doing so is perceived to offer more happiness? The system benefits the owners, not the workers. The more we buy into (pun intended) the current system, the more we are living from the outside in. This has repercussions for our health, wellbeing, life, relationships, and the planet.

Author and social justice activist, Audre Lorde proclaimed, "The master's tools will not dismantle the master's house." Although she originally made the statement to urge white feminists to examine their own racism and homophobia, and not to replicate oppressive systems, it fits well here, too. The master's tool to fulfillment under which we are currently living, is spending. Lorde suggests that we need another way. Mindfulness practices offer the potential of a more meaningful life filled with purpose, connection to each other and to the planet. Eastern communities have been practicing mindfulness techniques for millennia. For the sake of our collective future, those of us in the westernized world can and must learn from their wisdom.

One way to consider how the "master's tools" may have purposefully or perhaps inadvertently seeped into our sense of self and our lives is to mindfully consider who we have been taught we are.

WHO ARE YOU?

I often ask students or participants in a workshop whom I haven't met to consider for a moment how they might identify themselves – in only three words. Almost without fail, they immediately identify themselves by their personalities. I hear them say that they are funny, religious, caring, compassionate, among others. Some identify themselves by the roles they play: mother, father, sibling, daughter. Still others by the work they do: salesperson, technical consultant, manager, teacher, among others.

Take a moment to consider how you might describe yourself to someone who doesn't know you. What words might you use? Pause for a moment and consider what words come up?

Next, consider how people who don't know you might describe you, just based on your appearance. Take a moment to consider what words come up for you.

Finally, ask yourself if there was a difference between your answers for the first and second questions.

For most students and workshop participants to whom I ask these questions, their answer for the last question is a resounding "yes." In other words, the way we see ourselves and how we identify ourselves can be vastly different from the ways other people see us. Perhaps for the first question, you chose words that describe your personality? Or perhaps words that describe your roles in your life? Or your job/occupation?

For the second question, you may have chosen words that you have heard other people use to describe you. You may have even used some social identities (race, gender, social class, etc.) to demonstrate how you think other people perceive you.

For both questions, know that who we are goes well beyond the few words that pop into our minds first. We are much more complex than those reductive words. Our personalities, roles, occupations, hobbies, etc. are so much bigger than what we see on the surface. It is important that as we proceed, we bring our whole entire selves on this mindfulness journey. Please don't leave any part of yourself out. Let's be inclusive from the get-go!

Having said that, it is important to also understand the ways in which our social identities impact our lives. For when we start to recognize the importance of these identities on the lives we lead, the decisions we make, who we choose to hang out with, if/where we choose to worship, etc., we can start to see how our own identities impact the way we not only perceive, but also treat other people.

We are socially conditioned to understand each other based on perceived social identities. We all have a race, gender, social class, sexual orientation, and physical and psychological abilities, etc. When informed by the stereotypes we are taught by our culture to believe and buy into, these superficial social identities can make us think we know who someone is without even getting to know them. This has vast consequences in terms of our capacity for building relationships, especially across social differences.

Without minimizing the impact of our social identities on our lives and lived experience (more on this later), what if who/what we really are is even more than our personality, our role, or the way we earn a living?

WE ARE MORE THAN OUR THOUGHTS & EMOTIONS

We have been socialized to believe that everything we see around us is reality. If we see a chair, we believe it is real. I mean, we can sit on it, so our mind makes us think it must be solid and real. But what if who we are is even more than what our physical senses tell us? We'll explore this in the next mindfulness practice.

MINDFULNESS PRACTICE 3
The Observer

Find a comfortable seat. Notice your breath. Follow your breath for a few cycles, focusing on the inhale and the exhale. Pay attention to your physical body in your seat. Feel where your body is touching the seat. As you inhale, notice. As you exhale, see if you can settle into the seat just a little bit more.

When you are ready, notice your thinking mind. Notice all of the thoughts or stories your thinking mind is concocting. Perhaps your thinking mind is delving into the future – focusing on the things you believe you must accomplish, or the way you wish things would be, or an event or conversation you are preparing for.

Then notice your emotional state. What emotions are brought up by these thoughts? Stress? Anxiety? Fear? Panic?

Or perhaps you are thinking about your past: something you said that you wish you hadn't, or something you perceive as having happened to you. Then notice your emotional state. What emotions are brought on by these thoughts? Stress? Anxiety? Fear? Shame?

Or maybe your thoughts go to something more positive in your past or future. What emotions are brought on by these thoughts? Joy? Excitement? Love?

Now I ask you to consider: Who is it that is doing the noticing? Who is aware of all these thoughts and emotions?

What if The Noticer – the one who notices your thoughts and emotions is, in fact, who you really are? In Eastern traditions, this Noticer or Witnesser is also called the Observer. The Observer is the entity behind what you might perceive as the reality of you or who you know yourself to be. It is the calm, peaceful, nonjudgmental entity behind your thoughts and emotions.

If it is available to you, sit for a few more minutes just getting to know your Observer, especially if it is something new to you, and even if it's not. It is not bound by the stories of your past, the stories of who you are, the stories of who you should be, or the ways you should act. It is much, much broader than that.

Stay with that sense of who/what you really are: this expanded sense of the Observer. Some people experience the Observer in their head, others near their heart, or along their spine. Some experience it as an emptiness that is not scary nor does it produce a sense of dread, but rather an opening that has no limits or boundaries. This is also known by many names, one of which is Conscious Awareness. It is the one who is aware of your experience.

When you are ready, bring your awareness back to the present moment and back to your physical body. Notice your breath for a few inhales and exhales. Feel your body in your seat, and slowly stretch your body however it feels it needs to stretch.

Welcome back.

Feel free to journal now about your experience, or about any ideas or insights that arose for you.

The notion of the Observer is supremely powerful. It invites us to consider that perhaps we are not our thoughts; rather who/what we really are is the witnesser of the thoughts our physical mind has. We are not our emotions; rather who/what we really are is the witnesser of the emotions our physical body experiences. If you were unable to connect with the Observer, don't worry. Feel free to come back to this practice again and again. The Observer can be a powerful mindfulness tool, and a respite from all the chaos that we experience on a daily basis, in our minds, our bodies, and our lives.

ESTRADA'S HAND ACTIVITY

Here's another way to consider the Observer based on a TEDTalk by Juan Diego Estrada called, "Qualities of a Global Citizen." Estrada invites us into an activity that makes us rethink reality. He instructs: put one hand, fingers spread, right in front of your face, if it is available for you to do so. What if your hand/fingers represented your judgmental thoughts and emotions? You can't really see anything but your hand (your thoughts and emotions), and even if you can see through your open fingers, your view is partially blocked by the lens of the thoughts and emotions you are experiencing.

Now slowly, slowly pull your hand (your thoughts and emotions) away from your face so that it is about a foot in front of you. All of a sudden, your thoughts and emotions are separate from who you really are. They are still part of you, but they are separate. And they are not clouding your view of everything else. You can observe your thoughts and emotions, but they are not you. You are now open to see much more expansively; a broader, more nuanced view is available to you. Consider the impact this might have in terms of decision-making and innovation – being able to take many more variables into account.

These are some of the many benefits of the Observer. It witnesses the thoughts and emotions we experience, but is not consumed by them. Once again, the point is that who we really are is more than the thoughts and emotions we experience.

WE ARE MORE THAN OUR STORIES

If we are more than our thoughts and emotions, then perhaps we are also more than what we have been taught to believe about ourselves. What have we been told about who we are and who we are supposed to be? Have we been told we are too much, too little, too short, too fat, too overbearing, too loud, too … fill in the blank. We can choose to believe these stories about ourselves and live from the outside in, or not. We actually have a choice. Keep in mind, too, that when someone has told you who they think you are, their reactions to you have everything to do with them: their perception, their feelings about themselves, and little, if anything, to do with you.

When I was about twelve years old, a family member told me I was too selfish. She didn't just say it out of anger; rather she sat me down and explained to me all the ways I was too selfish. There wasn't an ounce of compassion, simply judgment. I have held that memory with me for decades, believing that that defined me: I am a selfish person. As a result, I spent many years working hard to disprove that notion. It was underneath all of my accomplishments. It was the hand in front of my face; the lens through which I viewed my world and responded to it. My motivation was always, "Let me show you how unselfish I am." And that worked well in this society where selflessness, especially for women, is highly valued. Unfortunately, it meant that any time I did anything for myself, I was wracked with guilt, because it proved what my family member had said all those years ago. Through the mindfulness practice below, I was able to finally let go of this idea.

Another example occurred recently in a conversation I was having with my mother. In the midst of our talk, she mentioned that she thinks of herself as a terrible mother. This is the story she identifies with. And after many years of processing my childhood trauma and cultivating forgiveness, I said to her, "You can choose to go through the rest of your life believing that about yourself, identifying with that story, or you can choose to forgive yourself, and see yourself any way you want to. It's your choice."

She was taken aback that I would say such a thing, knowing how much I suffered dealing with my childhood trauma. The truth is, I don't want her to feel guilty for the rest of her life. How would that benefit either of us? And I know it is stifling her. So even if her perception of herself has some validity, she can choose to spend the rest of her life beating herself up about her collusion in my trauma, or she can accept her actions, forgive herself, apologize if she thinks it would be beneficial to herself or to me, choose to behave differently, and move on. Although this can be challenging work, she has the choice to move forward. Whether or not she does this is up to her.

I invite you to consider what stories you have chosen to identify with that you, too, can let go of. We know that the thoughts and emotions we have, especially trauma-induced ones, are often stored in our bodies in various places. This next practice offers you the opportunity to sense where these thoughts or emotions have taken up residence in your body, and gently let them go.

MINDFULNESS PRACTICE 4
Unpacking Our Stories

Find a comfortable seat. Notice your breath. Follow your breath for a few cycles, focusing on the inhales and the exhales. Pay attention to your physical body in your seat. Feel where your body is touching the seat.

When you are ready, bring your awareness to your sense of self. How would you describe yourself? What words might you use? Are your first thoughts those of identity? Your job or occupation? Your role in the world? Your personality?

How do you feel about yourself? Are you happy and satisfied with who you are? Are there parts of you that you wish were different? Notice what comes up as you consider these questions. Spend some time with whatever arises. Come back to your breath and notice if there are feelings of comfort or discord in your body. On your inhale, focus on any tension in your body; on your exhale, breathe some air into those spaces. Continue this process for a few cycles of breath.

When you are ready, consider how you know what you know about yourself. Who told you who/what you are? How did you come to believe these ideas about yourself? Are they true? Is it possible that whatever you were told about yourself has more to do with the person who told you these stories, than you?

What if you could let go of just one story right now? Which would you choose? Pick one story and notice where in your body you have a sense of this story as being true and being you, or part of you, or part of your identity. Breathe it in. If you are willing to do so, you can simply express gratitude to the person who offered this perception of you, thanking them for providing you with a sense of identity, at a time when you were still figuring out how to be in the world. Then, acknowledge that you no longer choose to live by their

perception, and that you are actively choosing to let it go. Breathe. As you
inhale, focus on the place in your body that you have held onto that story of
you – and as you exhale, let it go. Repeat this cycle several times, each time,
allowing the story to unstick and dissolve a little more. You don't need to force
it out, but rather to accept that it's there and allow it to move through you.
And if it stays stuck and is not ready to go yet, that is ok, too. You can try again
later. Take as much time as you need to gently observe it, with no judgment,
just compassion and breath.

When you are ready, bring your awareness back to the present moment.
Focus on your breath for a few more inhales and exhales. Feel your body in
your seat, and slowly stretch your body however it feels it needs to stretch.

Welcome back.

Feel free to journal now about your experience, or about any ideas or
insights that arose for you.

You can repeat this mindfulness practice as many times as you have
stories you need or want to let go of. It can be a powerful tool of transformation. As the late philosopher and prolific author Dr. Wayne Dyer asserted,
these stories of who we have been taught we are, only exist like a wake
behind a boat. They are behind us, not in front of us. We get to steer the
rudder to forge a path ahead. Our stories, like the wake, don't have to have
any bearing on where we are headed.

WE ARE MORE THAN WHAT HAPPENED TO US

As we disentangle ourselves from what we have been told to believe about
who we really are, we are left wondering who, then, are we really? Maybe
who we are is a culmination of the experiences we've had?

Have you ever thought or told someone, "Oh, I am this way because of
something that happened to me in my past"?

We can use the stories that occurred in our lives to demonstrate how we've
been hurt. And these stories, our memories, can shape who we become.

Our histories do create patterns for us – usually as a mechanism to
protect us from getting hurt again and again. These patterns are very useful
as coping strategies. But often, we keep the patterns in our lives long after
they serve us. Talk therapy, behavioral change therapy, tapping therapy, and
other healing modalities are great options for unpacking these patterns and
letting them go so we are free to move forward in our lives in healthy ways.
We get to choose rather than repeatedly playing out the same tired patterns

involuntarily.

This process of unpacking and processing what happened to us requires the ability to forgive. The concept of forgiveness is extremely challenging for some people because they think it means acquiescing to what was done to them. That it was ok. But forgiveness is not for anyone but you. As I mentioned in the Preface: for-giving is really "giving-for" you. Spending time focused on how wrong the other person was, regardless of how right you are, is time you will never get back. Forgiveness to me means letting go of the spiteful anger, animosity, and negativity that threatens to eat us alive if we sit in it. I choose to live free of that hate. My choice. Once again, this may take some time and the listening ear of a good therapist to unravel; however, I can't express enough how freeing it can be.

In the meantime, as we consider those noteworthy, sometimes triggering events that inform our understanding of who we know ourselves to be, we actually have a choice in what we decide to focus on. Here's an example that occurred when I was just two and a half years old.

After my father finished a six-year assignment with Smithsonian Institute in South Africa, where I was born, and then a few years in East Africa, my family came to the U.S. and moved to the east coast. We rented a house on a hill that had a steep driveway. One morning in early winter, we woke up to the sun reflecting brightly off of a bed of freshly falling snow. My mother looked out the window and shouted for us all to come see. Excitedly, we rushed to the window, incredulous. It was the first time I had seen snow. As soon as the snow stopped, she sent us all outside to shovel the driveway. My father went out to the garage and grabbed a big shovel, and then gave each of my siblings (from the oldest to the youngest) progressively smaller shovels, and went to work clearing the driveway. My mother bundled me up in a snowsuit and sent me on my way with a soup spoon. I helped.

When the driveway was cleared, my father decided it would be a good idea to pull out the toboggan so we could sled down the driveway. He climbed onto the large toboggan, and instructed each of my siblings to climb on behind him. They did. I stood there beside the toboggan, frozen to my spot. He reached out, grabbed me, and shoved me between his legs in the very front of the toboggan. As we started moving forward, the terror gripped my gut. I felt nothing short of terrified. I started screaming to please stop, and was ignored. My terror only increased as our collective momentum increased. At such a young age, I had no conception of how to make it stop, so my instinctive sense kicked in and I put my foot out to stop us as if my tiny body could grind us to a halt. Instead, my leg twisted so badly, it broke. This was the first of so many times in my young life I can remember my body being forced to do something it desperately did not want to do, but having absolutely no power to stop it.

As I think back on this story, I could focus on the trauma I experienced, the pain of a broken leg, which was set in a cast for 6 weeks when I was just beginning to learn to run and jump. I could focus on the injustice and unfairness of being forced into a position and situation I resisted with everything I had, to no avail. I could focus on the fact that I had no choice at all. I had to be patient and wait until it was over.

When I was in therapy dealing with all of my childhood trauma, it was important to remember some of these instances, and there were so terribly many. It helped in my healing process to acknowledge what happened to me; what was done to me. It took me a long time to put a name to my victimhood, and when I was able to stop minimizing and denying the truth of all the torture I was forced to endure, identifying myself as a victim was a valuable stepping stone for me.

For a while through this process, my lens was victimhood. My figurative hand was in front of my face, and it represented victimhood. I could barely see anything else. It was the lens through which I viewed everything in the world – perfectly diagnosed as post-traumatic stress response. This was an important part of my healing process. Over time, and through much trauma therapy, I was able to take my metaphorical hand away from my face, very slowly, and see the abuse for what it was. My trauma. My torture. My experience. And most importantly, my past. I was able to use my Observer and see that I was and am more than what happened to me. I was able to lay it down.

I still feel a little vulnerable telling the story because it brings up those old feelings of helplessness, but now I can choose what to focus on. All these years later, when I think of that story, I like to think about the spoon. My mother gave me a tool for helping. That spoon represents what I now consider my super power! I have learned so many tools along the way – not just for coping, but for discovering my purpose in life, for getting in and staying in alignment with that purpose so I can continually be inspired by my creative spark, and soar! Learning for me directly translates into sharing any and all inspired thoughts, ideas, and wisdom with others. If you find any of it in any way valuable, it lifts us all up. As we each learn what we are here for, our intended purpose, and begin or continue to fulfill it, we are all better for it. It helps to heal the planet and all of its inhabitants from suffering.

MINDFULNESS PRACTICE 5
Finding your Gifts

Find a comfortable seat. Notice your breath. Follow your breath for a few cycles, focusing on the inhale and the exhale. Pay attention to your physical body in your seat. Feel where your body is touching the seat.

When you are ready, focus on what you might consider the gifts you have that you were either born with or learned along the way. What are your unique strengths and talents? Perhaps you are an exceptional writer, a chef, or computer technician. What comes easy to you? What have you always been told you do well? What are you most proud of about yourself? Spend some time asking these questions and listening for the answers to them.

See if you can come up with at least one if not ten things you would consider your gifts – what you bring to the table – what you have to offer the world.

When you are ready, bring your awareness back to the present moment. Focus on your breath for a few more inhales and exhales. Feel your body in your seat, and slowly stretch your body however it feels it needs to stretch.

Welcome back.

Feel free to journal now about your experience, or about any ideas or insights that arose for you.

Remember that your gifts are yours. No one can take them away from you. They can provide insight into your purpose in the world, but we'll get to that later.

So, if we are more than our thoughts, more than our emotions, more than the stories we were told about ourselves, and more than the experiences we have had, who/what are we really? This is what we will unpack in Chapter 2.

CHAPTER 2

Who/What We Really Are – Living from the Inside Out

"When you live from the inside out, it doesn't matter how chaotic the world around you is. You're at peace with yourself."
~Assegid Habtewold

I love going for a morning run in the summer when the sun shines brilliantly in the sky, and there's a slight breeze in the air. I usually run the loop in the tree-lined park near my home. What I started to notice this past summer was that I would be on the trail for a few minutes without seeing anyone, and then inevitably, two other people would come into view running toward me, spread out along the trail, and somehow, we would all reach the exact same spot at the exact same time. It's as though we were magnetized to each other. I had never noticed this before, but once I began to pay attention, I found it happened over and over and over again. So much so, that it's hard to believe there was ever a time when I didn't notice it. There is no obvious explanation for this, but anyone who has run on any kind of trail or track will likely recognize this phenomenon.

I began to realize that this could not be coincidental. We are social beings; we are drawn to each other. But even more, our energies are drawn to each other. We are magnets. And like attracts like. Have you ever noticed there are people in your life that seem to be so caught up in their own drama, that wherever they go, they tend to suck the oxygen out of the room they enter? If we are around someone's negative energy, we tend to feel down, and start complaining, too.

The reverse is also true. There are some people in our life that when they come into the room, we cannot help but smile. Their energy is so positive, it actually lifts us up.

This seems to be true whether we are aware of it or not. Once we start to pay attention to people's energy, though, we can see its effects. Recently, I was at a gathering at my friend, Jessica's house. We decided to do an experiment that demonstrated how energy has an impact on us whether we know it or not.

When a new person came to the gathering, we asked them if they would be willing to participate in an experiment. We asked them to wait outside for a moment before entering the gathering. Meanwhile, the people in the gathering were being given instructions. The instructions went like this: the experimenter said, "When I say the number 5, please think of the happiest thing you can think of: puppies, someone you love, etc. When I say the number 1, think of Hitler."

The new person would then be invited into the room, oblivious to these instructions. The experimenter said, "Five" and for about 30 seconds we thought all the happy thoughts and silently sent all the positive energy to the newcomer. Then the experimenter would muscle-test the newcomer: the newcomer was asked to put her arms out to the sides and keep them strong. When the experimenter pressed down on them, there was full resistance. The newcomer's arms were strong and held their position.

Next, the experimenter said, "One" to us, and we thought of Hitler and silently directed negative energy to the newcomer. The newcomer was asked once again to put her arms out to the sides and when the experimenter pressed down on them this time, they literally collapsed to her sides even though she was trying to keep them upright.

The newcomer had no idea what we were doing, but the results were dramatic. We all gasped. And it happened again and again with each newcomer that arrived, no matter which order the experimenter had us send the positive or negative energy. Although it was a bizarre party game, it powerfully demonstrated the impact our energy has on others.

I invite you to consider your energy. What kind of energy do you bring into a room? I am not referring to the negative energy that comes from being in a bad mood necessarily, because bad moods come and go. I am talking about how you tend to show up. What is your default energy? Now consider this: What if you had a choice about your default energy, and it had nothing, and I mean nothing to do with any external circumstances or situations you found yourself in on any given day? What if you could choose to live from the inside out rather than the outside in?

Living from the outside in means that you allow yourself to be a victim of circumstance. Your current situation defines how you see yourself and your life. I am not suggesting people have control over the horrible things that happen to them, or don't find themselves in really challenging situations or in excruciating pain, etc. But it begs the question: Why can some people be so positive even when it seems their situation is so dire, while others can be so negative at the slightest mishap? We could chalk it up to personality, but what if we could choose our response to any and every situation? This goes well beyond the power of positive thinking. What if we believed that everything that happens, happens not *to* us, but *for* us – for the purpose of learning and growth? This is radical acceptance of our life's journey on a large scale. Rather than getting caught up in the minute machinations of our brain's thoughts, we could have some perspective to *respond* to our life rather than *react* to it?

This is a framework for living a peaceful inner life filled with meaning and purpose. The path of using the Observer as a tool and stepping stone to experience conscious awareness is a well-worn path to alleviate human suffering. It is based on the teachings and experiences of so many philoso- phers who have come before, mostly eastern. I have remixed these ideas here since my students found them helpful, in the hopes that this version might be useful in some small way to alleviate even a little bit of suffering in the world. We begin by using the imagination.

Imagine that you are made up of a ball of light: similar to the sun, and just as bright – too bright to even look at, but deep down, you know it is who you really are. And this light resides inside you. It is a living light, not stagnant but dynamic. It makes you feel alive, excited about living. It has no beginning and no ending. It exists out of time. It has always been and always will be. It is a breathing entity that has no substance or density but its effect is very real. It is ethereal and at the same time connects you to every other living thing on the planet.

Imagine this ball of light is your Source, your Inspired Self, the Essence of who/what you really are. This is your conscious awareness: expansive and free. When our eyes are open, we might have a hard time acknowledging that who/what we really are could be anything more or different from the body we live in. But bear with me for a moment and consider the following mindfulness practice.

MINDFULNESS PRACTICE 6
We are More than the Bodies that Hold Us

If is available to you, close your eyes for a moment; if not, look down. Get still and focus on your breath. With your eyes closed or gazed down, try to feel your skin. Try to feel where your body ends and the air around you begins. If there is a breeze, you might feel it on your skin, but absent a breeze, it is very difficult to know for sure where your skin is. If that's the case, then maybe your Source/ Inspired Self/Essence/who you really are, goes beyond your skin!

Now imagine you are Light. And that light is so bright it goes well beyond your skin. Your rays extend in every direction; touching everyone you come in contact with. You are so bright, you reflect the light in everyone else. Your energy vibrates outward and when you are awake and aware of it, you notice people are drawn to you, smiling at you seemingly for no reason. How does it feel in your body to know this is who/what you really are?

What if you went through your day with this knowing, continually experiencing your conscious awareness? How might it change or transform your sense of self? Might it alter how you show up in any room you enter? How might it affect how you see or interact with others?

When you're ready, take another deep breath, and flutter your eyes open if they are closed. Stretch your body and take a moment to transition your focus back into the room.

Welcome back.

Feel free to journal now about your experience, or about any ideas or insights that arose for you.

Can you hold onto that sense of Light that is who/what you really are? Can you hold onto that feeling of expansiveness or conscious awareness, even with your eyes open? This is a mindfulness practice that takes time to learn. But I must say, it has the power to transform your life if you practice it and let it. Whenever I get stuck in the weight of a situation around me, and I remember this practice, it lifts me up and reminds me that there is more to consider than the details of this particular scenario. It is not about ignoring or denying what is occurring on the physical plane, but rather acknowledging that we are all more than what is occurring on the physical plane. This offers us a much broader perspective, and often, a sigh of relief.

Taking the notion of light a bit further, what if this light within you is a manifestation of the Universe or All Life? It is the place where your Passion/ Essence/Spirit resides; where when you are aligned In-Spirit, you are In-Spired. This light is the Source of Inspiration within us. Think about where in your body you feel it when you feel inspired to do something? That is precisely the source I'm talking about. And it is known by many other names: Inner Knowing, Awakened Self, Conscious Awareness, Inner Guide, Spark, Eternal Part of Ourselves, Soul, Spirit, or Who You Really Are.

Source of Inspiration: also known as:	Filled with:
Inner Light	Peace
Inner Knowing	Purpose
Inner Guide	Wellbeing
Your Essence	Happiness
Your Spirit	Timelessness
Your Soul	Expansiveness
Your Passion	Connectedness
Eternal Self	Compassion
Awakened Self	Belonging
Conscious Awareness	Gratitude
Who You Really Are	Creativity
	Freedom
	Love

Although we think of our Inspiration as an inkling about something, a whisper of an idea, our Source of Inspiration can manifest as something much bigger and much deeper if we focus on it. Our Source of Inspiration can present itself as a warm light within and around us. It is timeless and dynamic, and is characterized by a sense of calmness, peace, spaciousness, ease, stillness, acceptance, a deep, long-lasting excitement about life and living it. It tends to bring humility and gratitude for all that we are and all that we have in the present moment. It is not fleeting, but sustainable; not closed, but open/unbounded; not hard, but soft. Our sense of self is not based on what we were taught about ourselves and others, but rather who we are underneath those stories. Our Source of Inspiration is rooted in love, and it brings a sense of freedom and liberation that allows for the flow of our unique creativity, and allows us to engage fully in life; to soar.

When we are not in alignment with our Spirit, our Source of Inspiration can be overshadowed by our Ego; a/k/a our Shadow Self or Conditioned Self. Conditioned Self is all that we have been conditioned to believe about ourselves and how we are supposed to live. It is rooted in tendencies toward grasping, attachment, and judgment: superficiality, money, power, force, dominance, control, intolerance, aggressiveness, negativity, violence, stress, reaction, habit behavior. It has been known by many other names: "shadow," "ego," "darkness," "impulsive self," etc. Conditioned Self manifests as darkness or as a dark lingering cloud pressing in on us from the outside. It is where we are taught to focus our attention: to get caught up in minutia, "drama," who said what to whom, who is right and who is wrong, blame, arguments, etc., and the belief that the exact details of these things are extremely important. It is much greater than a personality trait, beyond just being egotistical.

Conditioned Self:
also known as:
Ego
Shadow Self

Filled with:
Fear
Shame
Anxiety about Past/Future
Contractedness
Grasping/Wanting
Social Conditioning
Intolerance
Need to control

Conditioned Self is manifested in the body and characterized by anxiety, nervousness, inner turmoil, gritted teeth, queasiness, etc. It can sometimes be disguised as excitement, though that will be fleeting (such as when you buy something fun). Ultimately, it tends to bring the feeling of "never enough," and an over-attachment to "stuff." Its focus is on the past (stories and beliefs about ourselves that seem unshakable) and/or the future (to do lists, and beliefs such as: "If only…, then I will finally be happy").

Conditioned Self was created in reaction to stimuli from our external environment in our human experience, with the intention to protect, and with a deep-seated belief that we need protecting. This part of ourselves is based in shame, fear, and self-loathing. Conditioned Self does whatever it has to do in order to avoid feeling those uncomfortable emotions; more so, to pretend to ourselves and others that we don't have those emotions. It shows up in our behavior as over-compensating, self-aggrandizing, over-indulging, and/or bullying ourselves or others. This results in a disconnection from ourselves and others in that it serves as a barrier from the truth of who we really are underneath our fears and shame. It ensures that we will not soften or hear that truth because in order to do so, we would have to feel uncomfortable emotions. Conditioned Self purposefully keeps us from learning what we need to know and understand in order to step into our best lives.

TWO ASPECTS OF OURSELVES

A tension exists between these two aspects of ourselves. Rather than seeing these aspects as a duality, however, perhaps we can view them as two pieces in the puzzle that make up all of our experience.

- Whereas Conditioned Self focuses on what was or what we believe (or have been told) "should" be; Source of Inspiration allows us to accept what is, in the present moment.
- Whereas Conditioned Self fosters a sense of impatience, chaos, rush, and feeling like there is never enough time; Source is calm, methodical, peaceful, and knows that everything unfolds in a way that is perfect, in a timeframe that is perfect.
- Whereas Conditioned Self insists on holding on with a tight grip to everyone and everything in our lives; Source knows people and things are fluid, they come and they go; holding on tightly is an illusion fostered by Conditioned Self.
- Whereas Conditioned Self makes us want to call someone out in a dis-agreement with an attachment to who is right and who is wrong; Source calls them in, meeting them where they are at, engaging authentically and compassionately with the goal of connection rather than alienation.
- Whereas Conditioned Self strives to control things that we cannot control; Source lets those things go, and focuses on our higher purpose where our spirit can fly.
- Whereas Conditioned Self grasps for tomorrow with a desperate sense of wanting things to be different from what they are now; Source accepts the present moment, focuses on gratitude and our Inner Knowing of our higher purpose, where when we are in alignment, opportunities present themselves to us without having to grasp for them.
- Whereas Conditioned Self considers the world from a scarcity model – that there is not enough for everyone so we should take what we can get;

Source sees the world from an abundance model – that through giving and service to others, we create more.

- Whereas Conditioned Self is contracted; Source is unlimited, boundless, expansive.
- Whereas Conditioned Self insists that we are not enough, that we are lacking, and that there is something wrong with us; Source knows that we are already perfect just as we are, that we have gifts that are unique to us, and that we can find fulfillment and purpose by sharing those gifts in service to others.
- Whereas Conditioned Self always wants more; Source knows that once our basic needs are met, we can be content with all that we are and all that we have.
- Whereas Conditioned Self is reactive, impulsive and reckless; Source gently welcomes new stimuli.
- Whereas Conditioned Self is rooted in end results and bottom lines; Source lives in non-attachment to the outcome, focusing instead on the process and the present moment.
- Whereas Conditioned Self lives in fear; Source lives in love.
- Whereas Conditioned Self views the world as hostile; Source views the world as welcoming and whole.

Our goal is not to rid ourselves of Conditioned Self, for it is a part of us. In fact, it is useful. It allows our Source of Inspiration to align with our physical body to manifest our deepest, most meaningful life.

Conditioned Self has an impulsive quality that can motivate us to action, as for example, when we mindlessly overreact to someone's behavior. We might at first try and justify our reaction, but upon reflection we realize we have veered off Center, away from Source, and are left with a sense of shame and suffering. As soon as possible, we can use mindfulness to return to our Source, where we can find our balance again; a homeostasis that brings a sense of continuity and peace. If we neglect to come back to Source, and instead stay in Conditioned Self indefinitely, we are less likely to live a life filled with meaning and purpose. As we progress in our mindfulness practice, we learn that living only from Conditioned Self is not necessarily what we need or what is healthy for our Spirit to thrive. Instead, we can approach Conditioned Self as a child that wants; yet who believes those wants are needs. Accepting ourselves means embracing Conditioned Self as a part of our being, and approaching it gently, with love, care, and most of all, compassion.

Conditioned Self covers our Source of Inspiration like a dark cloud so we can no longer see our Inner Light. Mindfulness Practices reconnect us with that light and bring us back in alignment with our Source, reminding us who/what we really are. These practices make the cloud of Conditioned Self thinner/more transparent so our Inner Light of Inspiration can shine through.

Consider it this way: if it's available for you to do, make a fist with your left hand. Imagine that fist is you. It represents your Source/Core/Essence/Inspiration, your ball of light. All it wants to do is be its expansive self, spreading its rays all around.

Now if it's available for you to do, flatten your right hand and cover your left fist like a blanket. This is your Ego/Conditioned Self. It covers the light of who/what you really are, making you believe that the world is a scary place. It makes you and everyone around you unable to see your Inner Light. In fact, its objective is to dim your light; to metaphorically silence you from speaking up and showing the world who/what you really are.

The more your Ego/Conditioned Self focuses solely on the evil in the world: political turmoil, climate change, wars, intolerance, exclusion, and the list goes on, the thicker that blanket gets. And the more challenging it becomes to see, experience, and know your Inner Light. That does not mean we can or should ignore the horrific circumstances in the world or in our lives – that would be considered Spiritual Bypassing, but we'll get to that in Chapter 3.

If you know your Inner Light or Source of Inspiration will never go out, no matter what has happened, what stories you have learned about yourself and continue to believe, what negativity or evil you perceive or experience in the world, then connecting with that Light can be life-saving. And as you begin to know that Source of Inspiration and trust it has always been there and will always be there, it becomes harder to ignore it. The more mindfulness practices you engage in, the thinner the blanket around your Inner Light gets. You are more and more in alignment with your Inner Guide; you are more grounded; and your rays start to shine so brightly, they touch everyone who comes into your presence.

As previously mentioned, the goal is not to ultimately get rid of the blanket. Our Ego is part of our physical self. We need it to get things done to fulfill our life's purpose in the here and now. You can no more get rid of it than if you were to wish away your right hand.

This framework for understanding these aspects of ourselves has been so valuable in my journey. Last year, I was teaching a course on mindfulness and social justice, and one of my students started going on a rant against a well-known political figure and his heinous policies that were causing so much suffering in the world. This normally peaceful, warm, loving student that I knew, in that moment, was overcome with rage. She was spewing so much negativity (founded or unfounded) that I was taken aback. I noticed the other students were leaning in, nodding.

I paused, took a breath, and gently stopped her, asking her point blank, "What would you do if he walked into the room right now?" Her immediate, impulsive, venomous reply stunned me, "I'd shoot him." And she immediately looked at me and around the room, nodding back to the other students, jaw clenched, expecting everyone around her to agree with her.

I took another deep breath and was able to recognize how her Conditioned Self had covered her Source of Inspiration. She was operating from a sense of hatred in that moment. I asked the class to pause and breathe deeply, and to notice their own reactions to her statement. Some students admitted that in that moment, they could see where she was coming from. And yet as we unpacked the situation using this framework, without judgment, students could observe how Conditioned Self can operate. Moreover, they could see how this political figure's blanket of Conditioned Self was so thick and heavy that his Inner Light was almost inaccessible to him or to the world. Rather than getting angry at this man for his actions, they could see he was simply the product of unchecked social conditioning that guided him toward actions that negatively impacted anyone who did not look like him, or have the resources he did.

This is not to say that we should not get angry or frustrated at the deadly system of inequities that exist in our society in the forms of racism, sexism, heterosexism, among others. These systemic problems, brought on by social conditioning and fear, must be challenged and eradicated. Though hatred can be a powerful motivating factor, it can do great harm to the one who hates. Perhaps we can use that anger instead to motivate us to take mindful action.

Rather than getting stuck in hatred for this politician or rage at his actions, my students were able to witness the situation and gain perspective, and take a deep breath. It was like hatred was my student's hand in her face;

she couldn't see beyond or around it. Using this framework of these two aspects of ourselves – our Inspired Self and our Conditioned Self – she was able to see the situation for what it was, and metaphorically pull her hand away from her face. It doesn't make the situation disappear, but instead it allows us a different way of experiencing it. It provides us with a broader vision of understanding, and of the powerful actions we can take to respond to challenges and inequities in the world.

These are some of the mindfulness practices we can use both in our own lives as a means of proceeding through arduous situations, and also to create and empower strong leaders and leadership in the world.

CHAPTER 3

Mindfulness in Context
and Spiritual Bypassing

You are an extension of me. You are not separate from me. When I see you,
I see myself. When I see you, I see my light reflected in your light.
~Ubuntu

We have all had times where we have felt disconnected from those around us. I felt this often when I was healing from trauma; as though my experiences were so unique, no one else could relate. As we focus on that sensation of aloneness, it can grow, and we begin to feel self-conscious. As soon as we feel separate from others, a vacuum is created, and all of our social conditioning flies into that space. Stories about ourselves abound, such as, "I am not good enough to have friends or be in a relationship," or we immediately go to stories about ourselves that we were taught to believe are true such as, "I'm too… and that's why I'm alone." Or we start to focus on stories about others such as, "That person is too… and that is why they are not befriending me; I don't even want to be their friend," or "What would other people think if they saw us together?"

The physical plane on which we live gives the illusion that we are separate. And this separation makes us afraid. It happens from birth. Once we leave the womb, we have the sense that we are alone. If we are given all the love and care and comfort we need, we feel grounded and stable. Many of us, however, were not given that sense of grounding and stability, and instead were left with fear. Boundaries were conditioned into us from fearful parents or caregivers who were trying to protect us from a fearful world.

Those boundaries are embedded in us, and even when they are "reasonable," can serve to keep our wings clipped.

We didn't have a choice about this as we grew and became socialized to the conditioning that was thrust upon us; but as adults, we don't have to stay stuck in that social conditioning: we now have a choice. We can help ourselves find freedom through mindfulness practices that provide us the grounding we need to be able to soar. In yogic terms, we call this "Root to Rise." The more grounded we feel, the less we are concerned with maintaining, or even setting, limits. We have the freedom to listen to our Inner Knowing, allow Inspiration to arise, and take action on it.

As my mindfulness journey progressed, I could see the benefit of having the ability to connect to others in a new way. The more I could connect with my own Source of Inspiration in my daily practice, the more I could see that Source in others. I began to see us all as connected through light and energy. I began to understand what some people call the Oneness of humanity; that we are, as many have said, not a drop of water in the ocean, but we are the ocean. And the ocean is love. We are that. Mindful liberation invites us into alignment with that idea; invites us to make that expansive connection.

MINDFULNESS PRACTICE 7
Expanding Your Light/Connecting with Community

Get comfortable in a seated position. Breathe. With your eyes closed or gazed down, focus on your inhales and exhales. Let go of any distractions that come into your awareness.

When you're ready, imagine your Inner Light, wherever you find it within you. You may feel it in your chest, your gut, your head, or somewhere else. Breathe into it. Imagine it grows brighter and expands on your inhales, and settles and becomes more powerful on your exhales. Continue with this process for several cycles of breath.

Then, allow your Inner Light to grow with each breath. Allow it to get so big, it expands beyond your physical body. Imagine that its rays extend so far as to reach the walls of the room you are in. And as you continue to breathe, the rays of your Inner Light breach the walls and extend to the edges of the building you're in. And then they surpass the building and extend out to the community beyond. Stay here for a moment. Keep breathing.

Recognize that you are so much bigger than the body you inhabit. And as you continue to breathe from this expanded space, imagine that other people in

your community are also much bigger than the bodies they inhabit. Their rays
of light extend beyond their bodies just as your rays extend beyond yours. And
know that there is enough space in the Universe for every single person's light.
And although you are a unique manifestation of Light, there is a connection
between every living being. We all have that light inside us, whether we are
aware of it or not. We are connected.

As you bring your rays back into your building, and back into the room
you're in, and back into your body, continue to be aware that our expanded
awareness, that expanded connection to others, is always available to you. You
can grow your Inner Light whenever you choose.

Stay for a moment focusing on your Inner Light that is inside your body.
Breathe into it. It, too, is always accessible to you.

When you're ready, take another deep breath, and flutter your eyes open if
they are closed. Stretch your body and take a moment to transition your focus
back into the room.

Welcome back.

Feel free to journal now about your experience, or about any ideas or
insights that arose for you.

The sense of connectedness to others can be quite strong. Once you
see the Source in everyone, it is hard to ignore. We forget this sometimes,
especially when someone is bothering us in some way. In my experience,
that is when the practice is most valuable.

Considering and experiencing our connectedness is a meaningful
and liberating practice. In addition to this practice, it is important to
recognize the specific context in which our physical bodies currently live.
The socio-political landscape in which we live has a strong impact on our
lived experiences. If we don't take this into account in our understanding
of who/what we are, we run the risk of engaging in what is called Spiritual
Bypassing.

SPIRITUAL BYPASSING

Spiritual Bypassing is the tendency to jump to spiritual belief systems in an
effort to avoid having to deal with our physical world, or our social conditioning. When we don't want to acknowledge or even consider the disturbing
news of the world relentlessly streaming in, spiritual by-passers say instead,
"Well, this physical plane is just an illusion, so social injustices like racism,
sexism, heterosexism, among others, don't really exist and don't matter."

This mentality can be tempting. For those of us who have consistent meditation practices, and have learned to perceive the light in every person, it becomes less important what another person's physical body looks like. If we are all spiritual beings in human form, then the human form seems less important.

Spiritual bypassers tend to put forth the idea that the highest form of spirituality should ignore entirely the physical embodiment of our social identities (race, gender, social class, sexuality, disability, etc.). This is problematic on several levels, not the least of which is that it can serve to silence anyone in a religious setting who speaks out against bigotry of any kind.

Liberation theology, on the other hand, connects spirituality and social justice. It recognizes that our social identities have meaning for us on the physical plane, and that because of those identities, some will benefit while others will lose. In her book, *The Way of Tenderness*, Zenju Earthlyn Manuel puts it this way: "We must look our embodiment in the face in order to attend to the challenge it presents. Only then will we come to engage each other with *all* of what we are – both the relative and the absolute, the physical and the formless."

Manuel goes on to explain that we are all raced, gendered, labeled, and treated based on those socially conditioned labels. In short, the skin we are in matters. We cannot exist separate from the social identities that we are defined by. Our lives manifest differently based on the lived experiences of those social identities. Much of the suffering that we experience is typically perceived through those identities, perhaps even because of them, and therein lies our unique spiritual journey. Manuel states that our bodies shape our spiritual quest. In other words, the embodiment of our social identities form the basis of our spiritual awakening.

To split the spiritual from the physical does a disservice to our life's experience. Our spirits or intuitions are encapsulated in our particular bodies. We all have a race, gender, sexuality, etc., and although they are socially constructed and have no inherent meaning other than what our society, and we, give them, they do impact our lives, whether we want them to or not. We are treated a certain way because of the way these identities have been given meaning. To ignore that dynamic is not only to ignore one's privilege, but also to ignore the fact that it is through these physical bodies that we are able to sense our intuition, our purpose, and take action in this world. Without these bodies, we would be dead.

Spiritual bypassing allows us to ignore our differences. It is a privilege not everyone gets. It gives the illusion that we are all treated equally in society, which simply is not the case. Although I will focus here primarily on the ways in which race and racism operate, from an intersectional perspective, feel free to apply the concepts to: gender and sexism; sexuality and heterosexism; social class and classism; disability and ableism; religion and Christian-normativity, among others. Although each of these "–isms" includes important nuances, they all can be examined through the lens of spiritual bypassing.

Ignoring race is known as *colorblindness* or *post-racialism*, and results in the denial of the very real experiences of discrimination that people of color face on a daily basis. Today, people of color continue to be killed, deported, and discredited, based on their race. At the same time, "colorblindness" or "post-racial" sentiments also remain intact. This allows white people to maintain their privileged status in society by pretending that race/color is irrelevant, and that we as a society have gotten beyond the idea of race. We have not. Nor should we assume that colorblindness is the ultimate goal for society.

It is typically from a well-meaning and well-intentioned white person to a person of color that we hear the words, "I don't see your race." They don't say it to another white person, but rather to a person of color. Clearly then, they see race. How can one build authentic relationships across difference, when it begins with a lie?

Most often white folks strive for colorblindness to show or try to prove that they are not racist, but the truth is, saying these words is racist. In fact, my research shows that those who adhere to colorblind ideologies are less likely to be culturally inclusive in their practices. This ideology leads to alienation and separation rather than connection. Even worse, when a white person erases the experiences and the existence of a person of color by saying, "Race doesn't matter," what they are really saying is, "*My* race doesn't matter, and so I don't have to face the fact that my race has served as an unearned benefit or privilege to me all my life, at your expense."

Whether you are endowed with white privilege, or male privilege, or heterosexual privilege, etc., living your best life means seeing all the elements of your life as they are, with eyes wide open. Denying an aspect of your life (like how your race or gender or sexuality impacts your decisions, your interactions, and your life goals) can severely limit your perception and your potential. As challenging as it can be, consider opening up to what you may not have wanted to see or acknowledge. Great gifts await by doing so, like deeper connections, a profound openness, greater understanding and empathy, and the list goes on.

ACKNOWLEDGING SOCIAL PRIVILEGE

I was an adult before I realized that my whiteness had meaning. As anyone who was brought up in the United States knows: if the topic of race comes up, it means people of color. I was taught that I did not have a race. Or that is what I would have been taught if it ever came up in conversation, which it did not. It was something you quietly and quickly mentioned in hushed tones so no one would think you were racist for bringing it up. Race is considered a taboo topic and if you simply ignore it, racism will go away. That is what our society socializes white people to believe.

When I first learned that my race had significance in my life, I was stupefied. When I learned that my race came with benefits or privileges that I did not earn, it took me weeks to accept. I did not want to believe that it was so. I wanted to believe that I had earned everything I had worked so hard for. I wanted to believe in the myth of meritocracy because it revered the power of the individual. Meritocracy meant that I was solely responsible for my achievements, and that anyone could get ahead if they worked hard enough. Anyone can pick themselves up by their bootstraps, right? And then I heard the rejoinder, "But you have to have boots to do so." And that idea shattered the ideology of merit in my brain. And this was only the beginning.

I began to see how my privilege operated everywhere I went. It all started for me with a trip to the grocery store. I had been learning about white privilege in a course I was taking – so the conversation was theoretical and academic. Then one day, it all became very real to me. I walked into a super-market to return an item. I held a bag in my hand that contained the item and the receipt. I went up to the customer service counter and stood behind an African American gentleman who was in the midst of being helped by a white clerk behind the desk.

As soon as I got in line, the clerk looked up at me, and by a gesture of her hand, summoned me forward. As I was in mid-step, my arms outstretched with my bag to give to her, a light bulb went on in my head. Before I could stop myself, the clerk had already taken the bag out of my hand and started the process for returned items. My face turned bright red and I was in shock. My mind started to race as I began to put the pieces together: Why had this clerk interrupted her transaction with this gentleman and asked me to step forward? Is this what being white gets you? Is this an example of my "unearned" benefit at work? I started to reel as I tried to think of what I could do to ameliorate the situation.

As I finished my step forward, I turned to the gentleman (who was now beside me) and said, "I am so sorry. I should not have stepped forward."

He looked at me and slowly said, "Lady, it happens all the time."

I felt nauseated and still stunned as this was the first time I had consciously been confronted with my own privilege. Given what I had learned in class about the importance of disrupting systems of privilege whenever we notice them, I took a deep breath, turned to the clerk behind the counter and said, "Excuse me, but can you tell me why you took me when you were already helping this gentleman?"

The clerk looked up at me, looked over at the man, and quickly looked down, silent, her face turning a deep shade of red. She was embarrassed that I was making the invisible, visible; that she had been caught. I realized at that moment that this is how privilege works. My stepping forward to be helped by this clerk represented the entitlement I had been taught I deserved, and the benefit afforded to those with white skin. And she had been taught, whether implicitly or explicitly, that her behavior was not only appropriate, but justified. You do not make white people wait. Our socialization tells us: our time is more valuable.

After the additional thirty seconds or so it took the clerk to process my return (yes, even after I questioned her, she continued processing my return), I turned to the man and apologized again. As I left, I was overcome with shame and embarrassment when I remembered that my very first thought as I saw the clerk summon me forward had been, "Oh good, I can get this errand done quickly" with no immediate regard for "at whose expense."

I could get stuck in the guilt and shame of having privilege and abusing it, but how useful would that be? As important as it is to acknowledge our feelings — whatever they are — we must not stay stuck in them or we risk perpetuating an unfair system by inaction. I did not create this system of inequalities. However, once I know about it, I have a responsibility to make the invisible visible every chance I get by disrupting white privilege, male privilege, heterosexual privilege, etc. As the gentleman said, these subtle and not-so-subtle slights, "happen all the time." They are known as microaggressions, typically rooted in implicit bias; two concepts that are covered in much more depth later in this book.

The era in which we live provides a context for shaping our Conditioned Self. At its best, taking this context into account helps us to connect to the legacy of the past and the generations to come. We cannot bypass the timeframe in which we are situated.

At its worst, however, taking this timeframe into account situates our lives within the system of inequalities and socio-political turmoil we find ourselves immersed in. To understand who we really are, we must also understand *when* and *where* we are. Otherwise, we are not living authentically, nor are we able to form authentic relationships, especially across social differences.

One example of this is to consider the land on which we live. How often do you consider whose land we inhabit? The beautiful land on which we stand, live, make our home, work, play, etc., has been colonized by white people at the expense of many Indigenous tribes. The population of Indigenous peoples on what is now considered U.S. soil used to be 100 percent of those living here. Now, as a proportion of the population, the number has been reduced to less than two percent. (And this minute number also reduces hundreds of tribes to one identity.) Through colonization, so-called Manifest Destiny, removal of children from their homes, cultures, and communities, rampant disease brought from other continents, and murder, among other oppressive and genocidal acts, white dominance has reigned supreme.

I use this example not to incite feelings of guilt for we did not create the system of inequality or white supremacy, even if many of us continue to benefit from it. This is not a blame game. We cannot alleviate suffering or challenge our current system of inequalities, however, unless we can see how these systems directly affect us. We must connect to the problem in order to find solutions. Once we see these inequalities, it is our responsibility to do something about them.

We are all taught misinformation about our own and others' social identities. We are consistently bombarded with messages from home, school, the media, our workplaces, etc., that serve to maintain the social hierarchy: allowing those in power to remain in power. These messages secure the dominant culture's status by perpetuating stereotypes that teach us to fear and look down on anyone whose social identities are different from: male, white, heterosexual, non-disabled, thin, educated, wealthy, and relatively young.

The purpose here is not to pinpoint the small percentage of the population that actually encompasses all of those identities, but rather to notice which of our social identities (race, gender, sexual orientation, etc.) afford us unearned benefits and a sense of belonging/inclusion, and which are considered "less than" and prompt a sense of "outsider" status/exclusion.

A PRIVILEGE INVENTORY

One way to become aware of how our own privileged identities operate in society is by taking a Privilege Inventory. Privilege can be experienced by: receiving the benefit of the doubt, access to resources, and/or a sense of fitting in. If, for example, you can turn toward the police for safety as opposed to steering far away from them for fear of an unnecessary altercation or worse, you experience racial privilege. If you can walk hand-in-hand with your partner without fear of being harassed or attacked on most streets in the U.S., you experience heterosexual privilege, or possibly racial privilege (if you are not in an interracial relationship). If you are made to feel welcome in most math, science, or engineering classes, you experience male privilege. And the list goes on.

Choose one social identity through which you receive privilege (being either white or male or heterosexual or non-disabled, etc.), and over the course of a week, keep a journal that tracks every time you notice how your privilege operates throughout your day. What are you able to do because you have it? How does it play out in your daily life? What can you do or access, that others, based on their social status, cannot? At the end of the week, review your list and write about how it feels to acknowledge the privilege you have. Again, until we connect to the problem of social inequalities that exist, we can do nothing to change them.

Some people finish the week and write about how grateful they are for the privileges they have. My goal is not to diminish that but rather to explain that those privileges, or unearned benefits, exist only at the expense of others. They exist because of a legacy of a deeply held system of patriarchal, heterosexist, white supremacist ideology (and by "white supremacy" I don't mean racist skinheads here, but rather the system of white supremacist ideology that glorifies whiteness). If you are benefitting from the system, it means someone else is at a disadvantage from that same system. It's the flip side of the coin.

On the other hand, keep in mind that whether we want it or not, we all have some type of privilege. We cannot opt out, because privilege is based on how people are taught to treat us. The question is: what can we do about it once we know it exists? A good place to start is to share this knowledge with others. Start a conversation with those around you and talk about it. Don't keep it to yourself. These conversations offer a path toward healing.

Also, the unfair and unequal system as it stands gets maintained by mind*less*ness. The less we think about privilege and white supremacist ideology, the less they are challenged, and thus, the stronger those systems become. Mindfulness, as we will see, is an invitation to recognize and dismantle those unfair systems. In this way, mindfulness is revolutionary.

CHAPTER 4

Mindfulness to Discover
the Wisdom Our Bodies Hold

"The way to your spirit is through your body." ~Ashley Asti

"Boys don't cry," "Man up!", "Don't be a sissy!" These are a few of the phrases we toss out at young boys to keep them within the confines of a very rigid box of masculinity. Although we live in a patriarchal culture where men are systemically given more power and privilege, at the same time, men are held to an impossible standard. Anything less than hyper-masculine behavior is considered weak. As sociologist scholar Michael Kimmel explains, "What it means to be a man is *not* to be a woman." His research found that boys' biggest fear in life isn't the fear of being physically injured or even killed, but rather to be humiliated or to be considered less than the strong, tough ideal our gender ideology insists they measure up to.

What are the implications of this finding? Boys (and later, men) are trained to channel all of their human emotions (fear, sadness, anxiety, frustration, trepidation, hopelessness, etc.) into the one emotion they are taught is acceptable to show – you guessed it: anger. I'm not suggesting anger is not a valuable emotion; it can help us to take action against unfair social systems, for example. The problem is when it's the only emotion a human being is conditioned to express, and it becomes the catch-all feeling, stifling all other feelings. Tony Porter, in his TedTalk entitled, "A Call to Men" speaks candidly about his own experience growing up being taught to hold in his feelings by the men in his life that were his role models. He suggests we consider the external implications of this policing of males in terms of the potential for domestic violence, sexual assault, in effect, all violence.

And what about the *internal* implications of keeping men in the restrictive box of masculinity? If a man has any feelings other than anger, he is trained to squelch them. In the westernized world, especially, we are all taught to hold our emotions in: to control them (can you see Conditioning/Ego at play here?). If a female demonstrates emotion, she is considered to be "overly emotional" or she "must be menstruating!" We are taught to prize logic and reasoning over empathy. This idea is depicted in Thomas Keith's film, *Empathy Gap: Masculinity and the Courage to Change,* that provides a closer look at the hazards and solutions to this gendered social conditioning. It's not that logic and reasoning are inherently bad, but when emotions are so severely limited, downplayed, and minimized, we are missing some potentially valuable information that we have been trained to ignore.

This conditioning is so strong, in fact, that it keeps us from thinking about or talking about emotions in general. Pause for a moment and consider what emotions you can think of off the top of your head. Take a moment and make a list of emotions.

What comes up? Happy, sad, mad? You may have come up with one or two more, but it is likely that it will take you some time to significantly add to that list unless you are in the clinical world. Once again, this is because if you were brought up in mainstream U.S. society, you were taught to rule your life through logic and not let emotion get in the way. We are cut off at the neck, using only our intellect. Our mind is supposed to give us the answers to all things. If we make decisions based on what our heart says, we are considered foolish. And if things seem to go wrong, we feel shame that we were too emotional, and we certainly won't do that again. We have learned our lesson! This, of course, is myopic thinking.

Because of this ideology that limits us from expressing emotion, we are not taught how to process emotions in healthy ways, and subsequently, we are taught that if we get help to do so through the guidance of a therapist or counselor, we are weak. The harsh consequence of this can be seen in the sobering and heartbreaking statistic provided by the U.S. Department of Veterans Affairs: each day, twenty-two soldiers suffering from post-traumatic stress commit suicide. That's almost one death every hour of every day. Something needs to change.

It takes a lot of strength and courage to overcome our social conditioning and seek out counseling. There are plenty who provide services on a sliding scale. I can attest to the fact that counseling was part of what saved my life. In addition to counseling, mindfulness practices provide so many options for health and wellness, and can have a broad-reaching effect if we are open to them. Let's consider some ways these practices can be used to transform our mind, body, and spirit for health and healing.

EMBODIED LEARNING

Using the mindfulness practice of the Observer highlighted in Chapter 1, we can observe our emotions and get a physical sense of them. We don't have to get stuck in them, but we can witness how our bodies respond to external stimuli. We can observe our internal reaction and gather a lot of information that informs how we proceed in the world: our response, the decisions we make, if we need assistance, among others.

In other words, even though who we really are is more than the emotions we experience, the physical embodiment of our emotions provides us with valuable knowledge. Our emotional responses can be roadmaps to living our best life with purpose and meaning; and can also help us to see where we are blocked through our conditioning, and what we need to work through. Our bodies can offer us insight into what matters most in our life, and can offer a doorway into powerful learning.

In my classes and keynotes, I invite students or participants to reflect on what they have been taught to believe about their bodies: cultural messages from home, school, the media, etc. Then I ask them to consider whether or not there is a connection between those messages, and how they feel about their own bodies. They are often surprised that there is, in fact, a connec-tion—people across many races and genders have tended to judge their own bodies harshly, to come from a place of lacking. And studies show that these messages start to permeate younger and younger minds—even in preschool.

I have learned that our feelings about our bodies has nothing to do with what our bodies actually look like. I have had students and participants who are completely comfortable with their large bodies, and others whose bodies fit society's beauty standards who are completely dissatisfied with the way they look. Even supermodels tend to be discontented with their bodies. After seeing herself airbrushed in advertisements, even supermodel Cindy Crawford exclaimed, "I wish I looked like Cindy Crawford!"

The standards we are measured against are so severely modified that they have become non-human. And yet, we think they are real. The underlying message is that we are not good enough. This has devastating consequences for all of us with regards to our self-esteem and our relationship to our bodies.

One of the activities I often ask students or participants to engage in is physically putting their hand on their belly. Interestingly, I get a tremendous amount of resistance to this exercise, especially from women. Our bellies are where we tend to hold our emotions, especially self-loathing. Playwright Eve Ensler found that the notion of holding our emotions in our guts crosses cultures – it is a global phenomenon. I invite you to try it for a few minutes and see what comes up for you. Even consider breathing into your hand to expand your belly and loosen the overtightened muscles there. Know that this seemingly simple act is actually revolutionary in that it challenges all that we have been conditioned to hold in.

We tend to store our trauma in our bodies, and the repercussions can be devastating. Much work has been written on the embodiment of oppression based on gender, race, sexuality, disability, among others. As one example, Ta-Nehisi Coates' bestselling book, *Between the World and Me*, spoke gravely and powerfully about what it means to embody a black or brown body in the United States. In an age when an unprecedented number of men of color are subjected to violence, and chained through mass incarceration, Coates ponders how to live freely in brown skin. He inhabits a body marked by an historic legacy of oppression. As beautiful as our bodies inherently are, society has bombarded us with messages of how we are supposed to feel in our bodies. We carry that pain with us.

One of my female students who was a trauma survivor, upon learning how her oppression and societal messages worked to shape her self-image in negative ways, started paying attention to her behavior in the restroom. Using the Observer, she realized that every single time she was leaving the restroom, she would stop at the mirror and scowl. She hated her reflection, despite the fact that she actually fit into society's beauty standards. So to challenge herself, one day, she decided to go into the bathroom with a notepad and a pen. She began to make a list of all the parts of her body she could not stand. And from head to toe, the list was long. She wrote and wrote. When she was done, she took a deep breath, and vowed to stay in the bathroom for as long as it would take to make an equally long list of things about herself she liked, or at least didn't mind. It took her hours, but from that day on, whenever she left the restroom, she would glance in the mirror and mindfully choose one of the positive items on her list to focus on rather than the negatives. This activity did not change the fact that she had survived trauma, nor did it minimize the violent sexism she had experienced, which must be addressed on a systemic level. It did, however, give her some control over how she saw herself, and it transformed how she showed up in the world.

What might it look like in your life if your self-image and feelings about your body matched the spectacularness of who you really are? What would that mean for you? Remember, this is a choice you can make and has *nothing* to do with what you look like. It is based only on your own chosen perception.

EMBODIED LEADERSHIP

I recently attended the Mindful Leadership Summit where there were a few sessions on Embodied Leadership. One was led by Richard Strozzi-Heckler, and he suggested that our body posture matters. Our posture impacts how we show up and how we interact with others. In fact, he said, "The shape of our bodies shapes our experience." If we have an open posture, standing tall and proud, we present ourselves as not only self-empowered, but also, open-hearted. This can lead to a more authentic, effective interaction with other people.

This theory is corroborated by Amy Cuddy in her TedTalk, "More Confidence in 2 Minutes." In her study, she found that if you stand in a power pose (like a superhero) for at least two minutes before a job interview, you are more likely to get the job.

At the Mindful Leadership Summit, Tiphani Palmer from Leadership Embodiment offered a mindfulness practice that allowed us to experience the positive impact that posture can have when dealing with a stressful situation. The following is my version of it.

MINDFULNESS PRACTICE 8
From Reaction to Response: Cultivating Openheartedness

Get comfortable in a seated position. Breathe. With your eyes closed or gazed down, focus on your inhales and exhales. Let go of any distractions that come into your awareness.

When you're ready, tighten up your body. Slump your shoulders, cross your legs and slightly lean forward, if that's available to you. Now tighten up the muscles in your face. Close in on yourself. As you continue in this constrained posture, bring to mind a stressful situation in your life. Something that has or continues to irritate you. Hold it in your mind for a moment, and notice your reaction. Notice how your body feels thinking about this stressful, even triggering situation. Notice what happens in your gut, in your heart, in your body. Notice any difficulty in breathing in this posture.

When you are ready, let the situation go, or at least put it away for a moment. If it is challenging for you to let it go, do what you would tend to do when your phone rings and you are in the middle of something else, and you have to answer it. Compartmentalize this triggering situation for just a moment. Shake off this confining posture in whatever way feels appropriate for your body, including standing up and stretching or twisting, if that's available to you. Shake out your hands or any other part of your body.

Now I invite you to get comfortable again in a seated position. Breathe. With your eyes closed or gazed down once again, focus on your inhales and exhales.

When you're ready, sit up taller if you can. Sit proudly in whatever way that has meaning to you. Perhaps open your chest wide, make sure your legs are uncrossed. Take a few more deep breaths and with your chest open, you will likely notice that you can breathe more freely.

Now recall the triggering or irritating experience once again. Hold it in your mind for a moment and pay attention to your reaction. Notice how you experience it in your body. Notice your breath. As you maintain your proud/empowered posture, notice how your body receives the situation. Sometimes this posture can even produce a compassionate, loving response to the situation that had not occurred to you before. Sit with whatever is arising for a few moments to gain the full benefits and warmth that comes from experiencing and living in open-heartedness.

When you are ready, take a deep breath, and flutter your eyes open. Stretch your body and take a moment to transition your focus back into the room. Breathe.

Welcome back.

Feel free to journal now about your experience, or about any ideas or insights that arose for you during this process.

You may not necessarily have let the situation go at this point, but notice the impact that various physical postures have on your reaction or response to the situation. It is likely to have less of a "sting" when we receive something challenging with an open-hearted posture. We'll come back to dealing with the irritation in a bit.

Notice too that our posture and body language is a choice we can make, all day, every day. Remembering to maintain an open posture is a mindfulness practice that can be life-altering – that is just how powerful it is.

More so, Vietnamese Buddhist Monk Thich Nhat Hanh talks about how even a smile can change your demeanor. I invite you to try this out. If you're not smiling right now, simply lift the corners of your lips. It doesn't even have to be a big smile, even a small change in the direction of a smile, he suggests, makes you feel lighter. And many social psychological research studies have corroborated this idea. Smiling has been shown to improve mood, emotional health and wellbeing.

This idea is also explained in Chade-Meng Tan's book, *Joy on Demand: The Art of Discovering the Happiness Within*. Like Thich Nhat Hanh, Tan's premise is that we can cultivate joy within ourselves, rather than waiting for something we might consider joyful to happen to us! This is possible with a simple smile. This tiny change can actually improve your own emotional state, your interactions with others, and can affect the decisions you make – in a sense, smiling can quite literally change your life. Throughout your day, consider the mindfulness practice of coming back to a smile as often as you remember to come back to your breath.

In short, our physical demeanor matters. We know the difference between meeting someone whose body language gives off a closed energy: arms crossed, physically, emotionally, and energetically withdrawn and disconnected. The chances that you will connect with this person is slim to none. And there is no blame here; that person may be having a tough day, but you notice they are not open to meeting you, or perhaps anyone in this moment. On the other hand, meeting someone who is open to you, who smiles in a welcoming manner, offers the possibility of friendship and belonging.

CHAPTER 5

Mindful Liberation

Right here in our bodies, in our defense of our right to experience joy, in the refusal to abandon the place where we have been most completely invaded & colonized, in our determination to make the bombed & defoliated lands flower again and bear fruit, here where we have been most shamed is one of the most radical & sacred places from which to transform the world.
~Aurora Levins Morales

If our emotions are not allowed to surface and be released in a healthy way, they can get trapped in our bodies, manifesting in harmful ways. This is not a new idea. Consider the health implications of holding on to those normal, healthy, potentially volatile emotions for years; for a lifetime. Think about the impact both on the physical body (heart disease, obesity, diabetes, other illnesses) and the psychological body (stress, anxiety, depression, other mood disorders). Notice, too, that many of these diseases are exacerbated by the inequities of access to healthcare which serves to benefit some and exclude others.

All of these diseases, if left untreated, can lead to the physical death of the body. Obviously, there are many factors that would contribute to these ailments, however, the westernized medical community is increasingly beginning to acknowledge that there is a mind-body connection to health and wellness and conversely, to disease and disorders. If we can see beyond our social conditioning, and acknowledge that a healthy body emotes a broad spectrum of feelings, we might be closer than we think to reversing some of the devastating health statistics in the U.S. and beyond. We must make it possible, if not mandatory, to include talking about and processing our emotions as fundamental to our developmental education.

A tall order, I realize. We are conditioned to ignore the important messages our bodies and emotions provide for us. We are taught to push those messages down and to avoid them at all costs, especially when emotional pain might be involved. And when we can no longer evade the pain, we want to skip over it and head right to redemption. We want a "quick fix." Consider the length of time we are taught to hold space for someone as they express their pain. Unless you are a counselor, our patience for the process is usually a few minutes. We might give the person a shoulder for a few tears, but then we expect them to pull themselves together and get on with their lives. And this is the standard we tend to hold for ourselves, as well. This was precisely my experience in recovering from my own trauma.

As I mentioned in the Preface, it took me awhile to acknowledge what had happened to me as an incest survivor. When I finally came to terms with those words, because of my social conditioning and my lifelong, very effective coping mechanism of Accomplishment (with a capital A!), I wanted to take a giant leap over the suffering, and claim the new identity of "healed" as quickly as possible. I found I repeatedly asked my therapist, looking at my wristwatch, "So how long is this going to take?" I would tell him, "I mean I'm willing to do the work to get through this, but I need a plan; I need a framework for understanding this, a roadmap to come out the other side, and an end date. Otherwise, I don't know if I'll make it."

He caringly looked at me and gently told me the truth: "There is no silver bullet for this. You simply have to go through the pain of it, and whatever else comes up along the way."

This was unacceptable. I quickly concluded, "Oh, he doesn't really know me. I'll find a roadmap, and get through this quickly." It was all I knew how to do. Make a roadmap and follow it, and you win! This is how I raised my kids. If there was something they wanted, we made a chart to figure out how they could work for it, with spaces for gold stars along the way for encouragement. If they had a project they needed to complete, we would make a spreadsheet with due dates. This is also how I was able to finish writing the bulk of my dissertation in only six months: I had a large whiteboard in my office that was color-coded with deadlines.

So this is how I first approached my therapy. I did my homework, read books, asked a lot of questions. I hunkered down, thinking I was ready to take it on! However, there was nothing that could have prepared me for the darkness that was about to descend. If I had known ahead of time, I could not have proceeded. And the truth is, it is nothing short of miraculous that I made it through those first few years of dealing with the depths of the pain. I had no prior experience to guide me. And I do believe a part of my suffering was brought on by the pressure I put on myself to get through it as quickly and efficiently as superhumanly possible. Turns out, emotions don't work that way. Who knew?!

FROM HEAD TO HEART

What it took instead was a veritable quantum leap in my understanding of who/what I am, and practicing again and again the tools I was learning from my therapists and my studying. Although I did not know to call it mindfulness then, I learned to slow down and pay attention to the messages my body was telling me. I started to connect certain sensations in my body with specific feelings that I could sense and name. I allowed the feelings to surface and finally escape. I learned that I am not my feelings. I just have them. And that those feelings are actually useful tools for healing.

I still have days when I have to remind myself of my practices. Every once in a while, I wake up in the space of scarcity and fear and shame and self-loathing. I am grateful that I can now fairly quickly recognize those feelings for what they are: a vestige of Conditioned Self trying to protect me from some long-forgotten story. Instead of living my life from this dark space, I remember I have tools to work through the feelings rather quickly, and come back to my true nature of lightness and joy.

What I never do is push those feelings away. As we are told by the great teachers: what we resist, persists. I learned this from my first therapist. But neither do I have to dig and dig to figure out why these particular feelings have arisen, or what exactly must have happened yesterday that might have brought them about. The truth is, unless there is someone to whom I need to apologize, the reason for my feelings doesn't really matter. Because whatever reason I come up with may or may not be true. After all, it's just a story and that story has little or no bearing on my feeling the way I do. We spend a lot of time trying to figure out why we feel as we do. Ultimately, it doesn't matter. It could be this; it could be that. And we can choose to agree, "Ah, yes, that's what it is." And that may alleviate a little bit of the anxiety – feeling like it makes intellectual sense, but the feeling is usually still stuck in us; in our bodies somewhere, and until we release it, it will stay stuck, and can grow more intense.

Suffering comes when we try to avoid the pain. That is the truth of suffering. We do whatever we can to avoid it; we push it down; we numb it with addictive behaviors because it doesn't feel good. In reality, no one dies from feeling feelings even though sometimes it feels like we just might; but people can die from resisting those feelings.

What if instead of shoving the pain down, we take a different approach? What if we transform the way we think of emotional or physical pain? What if it is here to teach us something we need to know to grow and learn? What if instead of pushing it away, we choose to radically accept it for what it is; even to embrace it? We could breathe it in and allow it to arise, and then dissipate. We would live healthier lives both emotionally and physically. As the saying goes, "Serenity is not freedom from the storm, but peace amid the storm."

If you need help in processing emotional or physical pain, don't hesitate to seek a counselor or therapist. There are counseling centers and other resources available even for people with limited funds. In the meantime, I will offer some suggestions here.

MINDFUL LIBERATION & SINGER'S THORN ANALOGY

As Michael Singer wrote in *The Untethered Soul*, we can think of our emotional or physical pain like thorns in our sides. Each thorn represents an old, disturbing experience we had in our lives that has stayed with us – stuck. It could have resulted from an experience we had as a small child or something someone said to us that caused us to feel shame, fear, sadness, or some other intense negative emotion. Singer suggests that now, every time someone or something triggers us, it causes what he calls a "disturbance." But it is not the person or situation that is to blame for how irritated we get, especially if our reaction to it is disproportionately reactive to the person who is triggering us. He says instead that the bad feelings that come up are the result of an old thorn being irritated.

When someone irritates us so profoundly, it feels so bad that we will do everything in our power to make sure we stay away from that person, or anyone like them. And because we have so many thorns from all the ways we have been ostracized, excluded, made to feel less than, etc., we can spend a lot of time and energy making sure that none of our thorns will ever get irritated again. We will try to control everything around us to avoid this pain, even if it means isolating ourselves from others, or ending potentially fulfilling relationships. Singer says that evading the pain of our thorns is the equivalent of pushing our thorns even deeper into our skin. Rather than alleviating suffering, we are in fact causing more for ourselves.

Singer suggests that as long as the original trauma is historic, and not still occurring, when one of our thorns is irritated, we have options for how to handle it. Rather than what most talk therapy suggests – to lean into the irritation and try to figure out where it came from and why it's still there – his recommendation is to simply lean away from it and allow the thorn to work its own way out. We really don't need to know where it came from, only that it is still stuck within us and is jeopardizing our potential for health and happiness. This process of recognizing the thorn for what it is – a remnant of a bad memory, Singer says, is the spiritual journey. And it is a challenging one because it means allowing yourself to feel the pain of the thorn. To allow whatever feelings that are stuck in us to arise. To breathe them in and experience them. But the good news is, once they are allowed to surface, as awful as it feels, those feelings begin to dissipate and once they are gone, they are gone for good. That thorn is gone. It's the stuckness of the thorns that causes our suffering, and our limitless capacity to avoid dealing with them. Liberation comes from mindfully processing them.

As yoga master Baron Baptiste reminds us, "Where the path is blocked is the path." What can you soften to, and allow to spring forth? Most importantly, ask yourself: what gifts, future, joy, etc. is ready and waiting to emerge when we let go of the thorns that no longer serve us?

Remember, it is useful to go through this process with a counselor or therapist as it can bring up some challenging emotions that, if you are not prepared for them, can be overwhelming. Know that you can halt this process at any time, and return to it later. Also, start with small thorns and as you build up this mindfulness muscle, you can move onto bigger thorns. Once this analogy is in your consciousness, it will become more and more clear when a thorn needs some attention. For now, start with something that has a small to medium charge to it.

Start by asking yourself if you are willing to let go of your thorns, even just one thorn. Acknowledge that although they are no longer of service to you, that they did, at some point in your life serve a purpose. It could have been self-protection from potential harm, humiliation, alienation, or something else. Most people don't want to give up their thorns because their thorns have allowed them to stay self-righteous. Holding onto our thorns has provided the false illusion of control, when really all we are controlling is the need to maintain distance from other people for fear of being triggered.

The question comes down to the old saying, "Would you rather be right or happy?" Here's an opportunity to transform your ordinary life into an extraordinary life. This is it. It is your choice.

MINDFULNESS PRACTICE 9
Embodied Healing

Get comfortable in a seated position. Breathe. With your eyes closed or gazed down, focus on your inhales and exhales. Let go of any distractions that come into your awareness.

When you're ready, focus on something positive in your life. It can be a person who makes you smile, or a pet, or an object that simply brings you happiness when you see it. Experience in your body the joy that this person, animal, or object causes in you. Notice your posture. Open your chest and your heart to this being or thing that moves you. This will serve as your anchoring feeling, one you can call upon any time you need it. Take a few more inhales and exhales soaking in the love.

When you are ready, consider a time when you have been triggered, something that caused a strong negative reaction in you. Preferably a time that was recent, but if not, a time from your past will suffice. Bring it up and sit with whatever comes up just for a moment.

As you recall the situation, focus less on the circumstances that made you triggered and more on the emotions that arise. Are you angry? Afraid? Frustrated? Ashamed? Sad? Anxious? It sometimes helps to put a label on the feeling or feelings that arise. Naming them can serve to minimize their power and intensity. Breathe.

Make use of your Observer here. You are not your feelings; rather you are watching your feelings. Ask yourself: where in my body are these disturbing feelings located? What do they feel like? Be specific. Name the sensation. You might say, "I feel a heaviness in my chest," or "My right knee feels tingly." Describe it: what it looks like, its texture, color, size, shape, if it has one. The more specific you can be, the more clarity you will have about it, and the less power it will have.

If it is overwhelming, stop for a moment and go back to your anchor: your person, animal, or object that brings you joy. Breathe into that for a moment. And when you are ready, come back to the disturbing feeling. You can go back and forth as many times as you need to.

From the Observer space, know that you are safe. If you are able to, see if you can soften toward the disturbing feeling at all. Don't resist the sensation even if it is unpleasant. Remember, you just need to let it do its thing. Don't interfere. Simply breathe it in. If anything, see if you can offer the feeling some light, some love, some compassion, even some gratitude for protecting you from whatever it thought you needed protection from. You can even offer it a hug and see what happens. You are conversing with your Ego/Conditioned Self here. Be gentle and compassionate if at all possible. This is very difficult and uncomfortable work – you are doing great!

Witness what happens as you are gentle with this feeling. Without interfering, allow it to move through your body and find its way out of you. Just watch and track it. Don't push it. Don't fight it – fighting it only serves to shove the thorn back into your skin. Allow. Feel free to use that as a mantra: repeating the word "Allow" to yourself over and over. Stay with it if you can. Take a break whenever you need to, but see if you can continue to return to the process.

If you can stay with it, there's a good chance the whole process will take no longer than ten minutes or so. You will know the thorn is working its way out if, after feeling the uncomfortable feeling(s), you begin to feel lighter and more expansive, rather than contracted and tense. Some people experience the feeling dissipate; others witness it leaving their bodies and floating away. Whatever you experience is your body's process. Honor that. If tears arise, don't be afraid to let them come. They are simply the result of an overflow of emotion that has been held inside for too long.

If you are feeling frustrated that things are not progressing or that the feelings are stuck and not moving through you, come back to your anchor for a while. You can even take a break from this practice and try it again later. There is no rush here. All that is required is a commitment to your own health and wellbeing.

Feel free to stay seated and grounded for as long as you need or want to. This is great work you are doing!

When you are ready, take a deep breath, and flutter your eyes open. Stretch your body and take a moment to transition your focus back into the room. Breathe. Look around the room and spend a few minutes focusing on the colors and shapes around you. Get grounded by noticing where your body meets the *seat you are in. Notice your breath.*

Welcome back.

Feel free to journal now about your experience, or about any ideas or insights that arose for you during this process.

I recommend working out one thorn at a time in one sitting; feel free to use this meditation process as many times as you need to. Part of my daily meditation process is to scan my body for any thorns that have been irritated since my last meditation, and to go through this mindfulness exercise to allow them the space and grace to work themselves out. It is a muscle that gets stronger as your meditation practice expands. The feelings that arise are no less disturbing, but I can tolerate them better mostly due to my now longtime practice and knowing that on the other side of the yucky feelings is an incredible sense of freedom and growth. And utilizing the Observer allows me to find some separation between who/what I really am and the disturbing emotions, so I am less apt to stay stuck in those emotions.

This process is the path to mindful liberation.

Check in with yourself now and see how you feel. If you don't feel any lighter, it likely means you have a little more work to do around this particular thorn. That's ok. You can come back to it. If you feel lighter, enjoy the feeling. You deserve it! This work can transform your life and how you feel in it. As you do more work, people around you may take notice that you seem lighter. This happened to me repeatedly. The more work I did in letting go of my thorns, the more friends and colleagues mentioned that I looked different, unencumbered. Don't be surprised if people start asking you what you've been up to!

GOING EVEN DEEPER:
MINDFULLY DISSOLVING SINGER'S "DARK BOX"

If it is helpful, the following is another way of considering how Ego/Conditioned Self has impacted our lives. It is also inspired by Singer's *The Untethered Soul*.

Imagine you are in the center of a dark box with no light coming in. Outside the box is 100% light. You don't know about the light because you believe that your life can be maintained by continuing to do all the things you have been conditioned to do in ways we have all been conditioned to do them (work, buy, work more to buy more). You stay in the dark box because it is what you were taught to do and you don't know any different. And every now and again, you come across someone who feels different to you – someone who has a sunny disposition, always sees the bright side, seems to glow from within. And you like their energy and may even be drawn to it, but you realize that being near them only seems to illuminate the darkness that surrounds you.

When you come into contact with someone whose light shines so brightly around them, something else happens, too. A tiny crack has been made in the box in which you live. And through that crack, the brightest light you have ever seen streams in. And as much as you are drawn to that light with every fiber of your being, at the same time, it makes you keenly aware that you are still stuck inside a box of darkness. As you are drawn to the light from the crack in the box, you start to notice how the darkness has seeped into your pores all these years. And you don't want to face that darkness, so you patch up the light and continue to live in darkness. Time goes by, years maybe. And eventually, when you are ready, another person or experience comes into your life that manages to create another crack in your box. Light shines through again.

And you feel ready this time to go toward the light even as it forces you to see the darkness that has seeped into your pores. And it is uncomfortable to see that darkness. To come face to face with it. And still, you allow yourself to feel the darkness for you have an inkling deep within you that feeling the discomfort might be a path toward freedom from the darkness.

And the more of the darkness you feel, you realize that it is simply made up of a conglomeration of past experiences. It includes all of the negative experiences you have had, all of the bad stories you have been taught to believe about yourself that have gotten stuck within your body, that have created blockages and ruts in your life and your way of being, and have stopped you from being all that you are. The darkness has covered over your highest self, your highest intention, and your highest purpose to the point that you no longer know who you really are or what your purpose is. And you only feel trapped by this when you realize you are in a dark box.

To actually experience, one at a time, little by little, some of the disturbing emotions that you have avoided most of your life allows you to pass through the walls of the box to the light, and it dissolves the box altogether. This is the path to liberation.

We are conditioned to believe that emotions, and especially tears, signify weakness. What a shame. Our tears are a great expression of the emotion we are feeling, and they also signify, as is mentioned in Mindfulness Practice 9, "Tears mean you have held your emotions in for too long." If we let the tears flow, let the emotion rise, we almost always feel much better. This is similar to traversing the edge of the dark box. It is yucky and does not feel good, but once we allow those emotions to arise and feel them, they almost always dissipate sometimes altogether and sometimes to some extent and we feel relief. Either way, we feel freedom from the trappings of our emotions, or trappings about the stories we have been taught to believe about ourselves, or our past experiences. We can get through to the other side – to the Light. To Freedom. To Liberation.

Moving forward always means letting go of something or some things that no longer serve you to make room for what is awaiting you. Letting go of the aspects of your life, like your thorns, that only serve to hold you back, allows for your future to unfold before you. Once you have had some practice mindfully experiencing who/what you really are, and finding freedom from some of your thorns, you can begin to uncover your purpose for a meaningful, fulfilling life.

I don't necessarily adhere to the idea that we each have only one purpose; for some, purpose grows and changes throughout a lifetime. Perhaps you were born with many gifts; there may be several ways you could put them to good use and be fulfilled. Regardless, in order to live a life of meaning, finding a purpose and living in alignment with it will bring about all sorts of opportunities and inspiration that goes beyond your imagination. If you choose to discover your purpose, and follow the path wherever it leads, you will be living a fulfilling life of meaning: free from social conditioning, and full of promise.

CHAPTER 6

Mindfully Living "On Purpose" – Finding Your Purpose for a Meaningful Life

"When the higher incorporates the lower into its service, the nature of the lower is transformed into that of the higher." ~Eckhart Tolle

I do not believe in New Year's resolutions. I have spent too many years at the gym witnessing the hordes of people pouring in as the doors open that first week of each new year. They seem so eager and motivated, and each year, I wonder if this time, they will stick with it. And inevitably, by the first of February, the default habits of those resolution-making folks have kicked in, and it's just the regulars who remain. If you intend to shift your life, why wait until a new year begins?

And so it was with the utmost surprise that I woke up on January 1, 2014, a few years into my mindfulness practice, with one word stuck in my mind. I don't make resolutions, so I wondered what this was all about. At the time, I didn't fully understand where it came from or how I knew it, but it was as clear as day that it had significance. I could feel the weight of it. The word was: *Congruence*.

I didn't know then the impact this word would have on my life, but it was so strong in my mind that I had no choice but to take note. All of a sudden, I began to notice the calming feeling I would get when my actions were in alignment with my values, and the dissonance I felt when they weren't. As my mindfulness practice grew, I began to realize that there was more to my life than the one I was living. Little by little, I started to yearn for that feeling of congruence – for the feeling that I was doing exactly what I was meant to be doing at any given moment on any given day. It was the first time I could conceptualize that my life had a higher purpose and I could align with it or be out of alignment with it. The choice was up to me.

Within a few months, I had left a thirty-year relationship with my then-husband, bought and moved into a new house, and began the next chapter of my life's journey.

Friends and family alike were stunned because my ex and I had had a wonderful marriage, and they could not understand why I would leave. They kept telling me how courageous I was to do this at my age. For me, it really was not a choice. I was listening to my Inner Guide/Inner Knowing, and it was telling me it was time to move on, and that I couldn't do so in my present situation, even in spite of my ex's encouraging nature. The only choice I made was to live in Congruence with my Inner Knowing. My choice, if you could call it that, was to follow that intention, knowing it would lead me exactly where I was meant to go, to fulfill my highest life's purpose. I am grateful every day for the freedom my ex-husband graciously bestowed on me.

That is not to say it was easy. It was one of the most difficult things I had ever done in my life. I truly loved him (and still do), and am so blessed to have him in my life. But a choice to leave? No. There wasn't one. Even during the one horrible moment of doubt that all but slayed me (but that's the subject of another book), I knew deeply that I was doing what I had to do – what was right for me. My trauma had followed me into my marriage, and after repressing the trauma for so many years and then feeling its impact, everything felt like a trigger. I knew I needed to leave in order to further heal and grow. Had I stayed in the relationship, I would have likely begun to resent my partner, and he absolutely didn't deserve that. I only ever wanted him to be happy.

And now I ask you: what is your intention for your life? Do you have one? Do you tend to go through life on autopilot – moving from one activity or appointment to the next without any specific direction? If you don't have an Intention or don't know what your purpose is, that is ok. I am not suggesting you must up-end your life in one fell swoop to find out like I did. That may not be practical or even necessary for you to live a fulfilling or extraordinary life.

But are you willing to let go of what you thought you were supposed to do? How you thought you were supposed to be? The life you were taught you were supposed to live? Conditioned Self can keep us trapped in a state of distraction from what we are meant to do. Wayne Dyer suggested we consider distraction as dis-traction: with no traction or motivation for moving forward, we are mindlessly living on autopilot, without intention, without meaning. As Cara Bradley, author of *On the Verge*, and mindfulness coach of the Villanova MBA reminds us: "A distracted mind has no power; a directed, focused mind has limitless potential." In other words, distraction ensures contraction. Intention ensures expansion.

In fact, a sense of purpose is on the top of Maslow's pyramid of self-actualization. Those who feel purposeful are living out loud – at their highest level. They are literally living "on purpose."

FINDING YOUR PURPOSE – FOLLOW YOUR BLISS

I invite you on a journey. Past your preconceived notions and past your conditioned stereotypes and stories, into yourself. This is a journey that unpacks who we have been taught that we are supposed to be and allows us to remember all that we really are. The promise of the journey is to uncover your own purpose; your highest intention for yourself so that you can live the life you are destined for. Rather than living from the outside in, getting caught up in the hopes and dreams that have been conditioned around who you are supposed to be, you can choose to live from the inside out, with the knowledge that we each bring something unique into the world that, if fostered can flourish and soar. Life will have enormous meaning and you will be fulfilled beyond your wildest imagination. This is possible, and it only takes a first step into the space between where you are now and your destiny.

All that is required is a willingness to receive and accept whatever lessons the Universe has in store for you. You don't need to travel anywhere or go on retreat or have a guru to follow – unless that is what you believe you need. I believe you have all the answers you need right inside of you. Conditioned Self has covered those answers up and we need tools to uncover them. Mindfulness practices allow us to slow down and listen to the messages from within rather than what our thinking mind and past stories have told us to believe.

Our bodies have so many messages to offer that can help us make decisions, and guide us on our life's path. I am not talking about "following your gut," but listening to the wisdom in your body. For when we do, it turns out, we can be in alignment with our highest purpose or calling, find our flow, and live a meaningful, fulfilling life. Once we find our purpose, we can begin to set intentions to manifest this purpose.

Here are a few questions to consider asking in the following mindfulness practice to gain clarity on your higher purpose:

- What kind of life do I want to lead? One that is superficial or deeply meaningful? (no judgment here, just a good question to ask your Inner Guide)
- Why am I here? What is my purpose?
- What is my intention for manifesting my purpose?
- How can I be, live, and remain in alignment with my purpose?

MINDFULNESS PRACTICE 10
Finding your Purpose: Getting Still, Asking, and Listening

Get comfortable in a seated position. Breathe. With your eyes closed or gazed down, focus on your inhales and exhales. Let go of any distractions that come into your awareness.

Continue to breathe deeply, and focus on your breath. See if you can tap into the stillness around you. As your thoughts arise, use the practice you are cultivating to just see them as thoughts, nothing to give your attention to, just observe them dispassionately, without focus or judgment. Come back to the breath and to the stillness that surrounds you, that is always available to you. Where your focus goes, energy flows. Remember that you can choose to focus on the thoughts or stories that arise, or you can focus on the stillness. Know that it is your choice. This is your practice. See if you are willing to focus on stillness and experience your heart relaxing, slowing down, opening up, expanding.

From this place and space, ask yourself: What am I here to do? What is my life's purpose? Pause. Breathe. Don't demand an answer, just sit in the stillness and allow yourself to receive your inner wisdom. You may "hear" the question reflected back to you: What IS my life's purpose? Sometimes, that's when the insight comes. Don't think of an answer. Allow the answer to come from within you. What do you know for sure? What is so solid inside you that you instinctively know it is True for you? What makes you feel expanded rather than contracted? If you get a sense of what you should do, just let that come up and let it go: that is your thinking mind, not your Inspired Self. Sit and gently listen some more with an expanded awareness of patience, openness, and a willingness to receive. Breathe. Allow.

Do your best not to second-guess or doubt what comes up. Our Conditioned Self is right there, waiting to shed doubt on anything that arises. Gently offer gratitude to Conditioned Self for its protective skepticism and allow your inner wisdom to be heard. Turn down the volume of your Conditioned Self and turn up the volume of your Inspired Self.

Sit and listen. What does it have to say to you? What knowledge can it offer that it has perhaps never or hardly ever been given the opportunity to share? Be patient. It can be very shy from years of being silenced. Allow the voice to surface. You can even have a gentle conversation with it, asking: What would you like me to know?

You might be surprised by what surfaces. It could be a very subtle sensation in your body. A whisper or a tingling somewhere in your body. Sit with it and allow it to share its wisdom with you.

If nothing surfaces, there is no need to feel frustrated. Remember that this is a practice. Tell yourself that this was a good start. And you can engage in this practice as many times as you like. Be patient. This is not something we are taught to do. We are all learning.

When you are ready, take a deep breath, and flutter your eyes open. Stretch your body and take a moment to transition your focus back into the room. Breathe.

Welcome back.

Feel free to journal now about your experience, or about any ideas or insights that arose for you during this process.

Again, feel free to repeat this mindfulness practice as many times as you like. It is a wonderful practice to start to gain access to your Inner Knowing. If you don't "hear" any messages at this point, don't worry. It can take time to cultivate this question and answer practice. Listening is more of an art than a science, but over time you will come to see that it works. It will not fail you.

Whenever you are struggling with a difficult decision, or even a minor decision, practice checking in with your body to find answers. This mindfulness practice is like a muscle you can strengthen as you go. You will know you are on the right track if you go towards whatever insight comes that makes you feel even just a little bit more expanded or lighter in your chest or body. Continue in that direction. The answers are there. And if you feel it in a different way, great, you do you. Just go with whatever tends to feel better rather than what doesn't feel as good within your body. Joseph Campbell recommends we follow our bliss. The feeling of bliss is a great indicator that we are headed in the direction of our deeper purpose.

Once you know your life's purpose, there is only one choice after that: Which path will I follow – the path that is *in alignment* with my life's purpose or the one that is *out of alignment* with my life's purpose? Will I choose to live in the flow or out of it? Feeling expanded or contracted? Chances are, you have already seen what it's like to live out of alignment. How has that worked for you so far? Perhaps it's time to try something different? To make a different choice?

What does it mean to break free? To live to your heart's content? For me, that feeling of freedom has surpassed anything I've ever experienced before. I feel lifted up, empowered to show up exactly as I am. It feels like a full expression of love.

Take a moment to explore what that might feel like for you. Not to feel bounded or restricted by society's expectations of you. What are you noticing?

Creativity is what happens when we are free to be ourselves fully. Inspiration is when we are allowed to connect with our insight and we can share it, from an unconditioned space, without the reductive logic and thinking that serve to diminish the inspiration, and in effect, us.

Conditioning can squelch the creative self and the creative process. Conditioning shrinks us, makes us contract, and makes us less than we are. If we are coming from conditioned space, we aren't free to be who we really are. We cannot connect to our higher purpose because we are constantly critiquing ourselves. Conditioned thinking is the opposite of brainstorming. We need the lightning and thunder of brainstorming to drown out restrictive logic so we can share our divinely inspired ideas that come from our highest self.

A DESIRE INVENTORY

Several months back, I was invited to my friend Jamal's house to dream. He is someone who works with corporations to map out where they want to go with their companies and how to work backwards to make those goals come to fruition. He asked me to write a statement about my life aspirations and desires. I had never thought to do this before for two reasons. First, with all the trauma I had experienced, I had never envisioned myself having a long future. I couldn't think a year ahead let alone 5 or 10 years. Second, I did not want to think big because I had finally come to a place in which I felt the Universe would take care of me, and I felt selfish asking for things. That was partly because I am not sure I believed I deserved anything special (that was Conditioned Self telling me I am not enough!), and partly because I didn't want to get too specific for fear my desires wouldn't come to fruition and I would be disappointed. Also, I wanted to leave my dreams open so that even bigger things could show up!

Yet I was being asked to think about what I truly wanted, and as I started to write ideas down on Jamal's gigantic white board, he kept saying, "Think Bigger!" and would walk out of the room, allowing me time just simply to dream.

So what did I do? You guessed it, I began a new mindfulness practice, which I will share below… and dream I did. By the time we were done for the day, I had filled the white board with ideas and goals. I couldn't sleep that night and many nights after that because I could not wait to wake up and start making everything happen! I had no idea there was so much I wanted to do. (One of them was writing this book, by the way.)

The best part was that each one of my goals/desires came from my Inner Guide, and I had a feeling of expansion and a deep knowing that each item on the list and more would come to pass. I knew that taking one step forward would set a ball in motion that would open up all kinds of opportunities that I had never before imagined. These ideas did not come out of my small-thinking, superficial Conditioned Self. They came from a much deeper place inside me – from Inspired Self. I began to acknowledge that we are meant for so much more than most of us are taught we are.

Now that you have some clarity about what your higher purpose is, this is your opportunity to think big! Consider what you would like your life to look like if you were living your ideal life. Who would be included? Who might not be? What might you be doing with your time? What might your average day look like? What part of the world would you be living in? What kind of home would you live in? What does it feel like? Generate that excitement within you and Think Big! This is your chance to dream!

Be mindful of the fact that this is not about what you can own or acquire in your life. That is living small. Consider a much deeper sense of joy than what your Conditioned Self can conjure. Sit in the feeling of your ultimate bliss.

Get comfortable in a seated position. Breathe. With your eyes closed or gazed down, focus on your inhales and exhales. Let go of any distractions that come into your awareness.

Continue to breathe and with every inhale and exhale, begin to relax just a little bit more. Notice how your body feels in this moment. Notice your energy. See if you can extend the exhales to be a bit longer than your inhales. This calms the parasympathetic nervous system. Do not force the breath; gently find some peace and stillness. If you are having a hard time calming yourself, focus on where in your body you feel any anxious energy, and breathe into that area. As you inhale, breathe in the disturbed energy, and as you exhale, gently say, "Release." Continue this process until you feel a sense of calm.

When you are ready, in the stillness, invite yourself to consider the following questions. Ask each question and wait to see if you hear or sense some kind of response from deep within before moving ahead to the next question. Check in and make sure that the responses are coming from your Inner Knowing or your heart, as opposed to coming from a thought in your head. Gently open yourself to receiving whatever arises. This is your Desire Inventory.

- *What do I want?*
- *How am I meant to manifest my highest purpose?*
- *How can I move toward my goals with maximum joy in my life?*
- *What might my best life look like?*
- *What might my best life feel like?*

Take a moment to dream. What if you could move forward with your higher purpose? What might it feel like to spread your wings and fly? What might it feel like to live a life where you wake up every morning so excited by your choices? You are ready to take on the world! You are ready to soar! Stave off your Conditioned Self that might be interfering with your dream or minimizing it, or telling you why it is not possible, and just sit with that positive, inspired feeling for as long as you like. Relish the feeling.

When you are ready, take a deep breath, and flutter your eyes open. Stretch your body and take a moment to transition your focus back into the room. Breathe.

Welcome back.

Feel free to journal now about your experience, or about any ideas or insights that arose for you during this process.

Take some time to write down as many ideas as you can think of that came up for you during this mindfulness practice. Simply brainstorm. Do not hold back. Do not worry about what is ultimately possible for you, or the reasons why you can't do something. Simply dream, and dream big. Your ideas will lead you to even more, bigger ideas. Don't let any thought or limiting belief interfere with your list. Dare to dream!

This process shifted my perspective of my life. Why would I continue to live small when I could choose instead to live large? Yes, we all have realities of life that might make it take longer to reach our dreams, but if we don't give ourselves the opportunity to consider the possibilities, we will continue to live much smaller lives than we could be living. And the truth is, once these ideas are in your head, any single step you take toward even one of those goals allows the Universe to provide momentum that you never would have imagined before. My mantra since that day in Jamal's house, when I accepted the opportunity to dream, is: Why Not?

Once I had my list of dreams/desires, my brain started conjuring up scenarios that I had never before considered, illuminating how I might get from where I was to where I wanted to go. A path began to form before my feet. All I had to do was to take one step in that direction and the wind would carry me. I began to set some intentions for the direction I was headed.

SETTING INTENTIONS

Through my daily meditations, I began to ask for and receive from my Inner Guide/Inner Wisdom a daily intention. Most often it was the intention to connect with my Inspired Self as often as possible throughout the day. Some other intentions that arose were: To stay mindful of my higher purpose. To be of service. To remember to raise my own consciousness when I feel my energy has become trapped in Conditioned Self. To mindfully raise the consciousness of those around me by cultivating and sharing positive energy. To cultivate joy in my life and share that joy with others.

What might your intentions be? Now that you have some ideas about what you want your life to be like, what might be some intentions that would be one step in the direction of making one of your dreams/desires come to fruition? You don't need to have a plan for all of what you envision; you only need one action you can take that puts you in the direction of that vision. For me, as I mentioned, one of those intentions was to write this book. I had been contemplating it for a few years, but after that day that I got to conjure a list of my dreams, I realized there were quite a few things on my list I couldn't do right away, or that I had no control over, but the one thing I knew I could do was to sit down and write. And I did.

Consider the list you created. Of all the ideas you have, choose one dream/desire you could begin to create or put into practice today. What is one action you can take? Set an intention to do so. Perhaps it feels right to you to create a vision board. Perhaps you want to put sticky notes up on your bathroom mirror with this intention. Perhaps you want to set a reminder of your intention on your phone to go off every hour you are awake. Whatever it takes to keep your thoughts and energy focused on your idea. This is how we stay in the creative zone. Again, remember that where your focus goes, energy flows.

Just remember that to live a life on purpose, the energy must come from your Source of Inspiration, not your Conditioned Self. If moving forward in the direction of your dreams gets overwhelming or overly stressful, the dream may be originating from Conditioned Self. Pause and reflect. Ask yourself: Does this dream/desire feel expansive and joyful to me? Does it make me feel lighter? These are typically signs that you are headed in a good direction. If, on the other hand, the desire brings a heavy feeling like you would have to push and push to make it happen, then the desire is likely coming from Conditioned Self.

When you are living in the realm of possibility from Inspired Self, you know you are living your best life. People around you begin to notice and are drawn to your positive energy. That's when the magic starts to happen because people you might not otherwise have met begin to show up, and doors start to open for you. You are on your way!

CHAPTER 7

Mindfully Discovering What Stops Us

"Sometimes it's the journey that teaches you a lot about your destination."
~Drake

I spent the last few years in a deep sense of transition. I sensed momentum growing within me. I knew that I was about to take off. I repeatedly told friends that I felt like I was on a springboard, and that I was ready to leap forward. I stayed on that springboard for quite some time, waiting (often impatiently) for my time to come. At some point, I made the shift. I cannot recall an exact time or day, but I could feel a difference. I was no longer waiting. I had decided to simply go for it. But it did not happen by accident or by coincidence. It took some work to discover what was holding me back from taking that leap.

Once we have released some of our thorns, and uncovered our greater purpose, dared to dream, and set some intentions, it is not yet smooth sailing. We still have one more important step: to discover some of the roadblocks that keep us from moving forward. Here are a few of the most common roadblocks that I, and some of the clients I coach, typically experience.

INSECURITY VS. CREATIVITY

When I first dared to dream, and make my Desire Inventory list, Conditioned Self shot me down with each item I wrote. Who am I to want a house on a beach from where I could see, hear, and smell the ocean? I became self-conscious and insecure. Conditioned Self was telling me I should write "social justice" on my list, not something so selfish as a beach house. And yes, from the bottom of my heart, I want that too, and it is ok to want both of those things at the same time, so I included both on my list!

Reflect upon the process of creating your Desire Inventory. Was it difficult for you to acknowledge what you want? Did you notice yourself, at least at first, limiting yourself with reasons why you can't have this, or why you shouldn't want that? This is Conditioned Self interfering with your Inspired Self. Conditioned Self is rooted in stories we were taught about ourselves; stories that make us feel shame, guilt, and certainly self-conscious and insecure.

When Conditioned Self arises, we can mindfully choose to focus on the moment, on our breath if that helps. We cannot be present in the moment and insecure at the same time. When we are present, the stories subside, as though the volume of Conditioned Self is turned down, and we can turn up and tune in to Inspired Self, where creativity is welcome.

SCARCITY VS. ABUNDANCE

One of my coaching clients, Danita and I were in the middle of a session recently. She is a realtor in the Midwest and is the primary earner in her family. She constantly feels the pressure of maintaining her household, which includes her spouse and child. She has attended leadership and sales seminars and created a vision board. Although she returned home inspired from these events, she still struggled, unsure when her next sale would happen, and worried that her income would not be enough to put food on the table.

What she said to me was, "I feel like I'm constantly in survival mode, and I'll never get beyond it."

Without trying to minimize or make light of her situation in any way, I reminded her that we have a choice about how we perceive our situation, no matter how dire it may be. I am not suggesting that changing our perception will magically put food on the table, or alter the reality of a life in poverty, or eradicate racism; rather, even if you are currently living paycheck to paycheck, shifting your mentality from scarcity to abundance, recognizing and articulating the abundances you do have, offers a more optimistic outlook for the future, which research shows can lead to an increase in health and wellness. I asked her if she was aware that she was living in Scarcity mode rather than Abundance mode.

Living in the perspective of scarcity means you consider there is a finite amount of success/wealth/happiness, etc. in the world, and you have to fight to gain access to your piece of the pie. It creates an environment of competition rather than cooperation. There is nothing inherently wrong with healthy competition; however, if it impinges on your beliefs about yourself or your enjoyment of life, it can become problematic. This mentality can also lead to envy when someone else gets what you desperately want. Rather than being happy for them, and taking it as an opportunity to remember and be excited about your own list of desires, the seeds of animosity grow and fester. People who live in scarcity often sacrifice their health (no time to sleep, eat well, or exercise) and well-being (no time to enjoy life) in the name of work. Scarcity also breeds a shorter lifespan, operating from a place of fear and lack – from Conditioned Self.

Those who operate from an Abundance mentality, on the other hand, trust that the Universe has their back. Unless you are living in survival mode right now, rather than metaphorically fighting the Universe for scraps, Gabrielle Bernstein, author of *The Universe Has Your Back*, suggests, "Allow the Universe to provide you with what you asked for" – we can ask and then we must be open to receiving.

Asking the Universe for what you long for is a beautiful practice. Asking puts your desires into the Universe so all that you would like to manifest in your life is made clear. Asking from a place of scarcity or lack, breeds more scarcity. Asking from a place of abundance, however, breeds more abundance. Once we ask from a place of fullness and gratitude, we are already on our way. We ask and then release the desire knowing it will manifest. And then rather than getting stuck in worry about when the desire will happen, we take a step in the direction of bringing it about. Not a push, but rather a pull to what you are drawn to do next!

How do we shift from a mindset of Scarcity to Abundance? One of the best ways to start is to acknowledge that we have somehow landed in Scarcity mode. Sometimes it is all we need in order to wake up to who we really are. As Marianne Williamson wisely reminds us in *The Gift of Change*, "Who we really are is a power bigger than all our problems, both personal and collective. And when we have remembered who we are, our problems – which are literally nothing more than manifestations of our forgetfulness – will disappear."

Oftentimes, we are so stuck in Conditioned Self, we don't even realize that is where we have landed. Sometimes this sense of lack can stay with us for hours, days, weeks, even years. I'm sure you have met people who give off this negative "victim" energy. Again, this is not to say they haven't been through some genuinely difficult struggles or challenges. The mark of an awakened soul is how quickly we can shift from Scarcity to Abundance. This is the measure of our level of consciousness.

Again, when you find yourself in Scarcity, simply remember that this is not who you really are. This is just a representation of some challenges your body is currently experiencing, an opportunity to breakthrough rather than breakdown. This is a great chance to consider your limiting beliefs – those notions that hold us back from living our best life. What is keeping you from receiving all that the Universe is waiting to provide? We stay small if we make choices based on the energy of Conditioned Self, and also when we get consumed by other people's perceptions of us.

NOTICING OTHER PEOPLE'S REACTIONS

"You're doing what?"

When I told friends and family that I was leaving the university to consult fulltime after recently having been awarded tenure, their reactions gave me so much insight into where they were coming from. The first person I told responded incredulously, as though a vital screw had come unhinged in my brain, leaving me on the verge of total collapse. "How could you leave a stable job of almost twenty years with no job to go to?!" he demanded. His fear was palpable, even over the phone. So strong, in fact, that it made me nervous. Was I making a mistake? What was I thinking? How will I survive? I started to go with him down this very, very dark rabbit hole of doubt. I was sinking into an abyss of reductive, contracted energy.

And suddenly, I knew I had to get off the phone. Although I know he truly had my best interest at heart, and wanted to make sure I was not being rash or doing something impulsive that I would regret, it was clouded with such a sense of gloom and negativity, I had to disengage as quickly as I could.

My head was still spinning when I hung up and for a while thereafter, but when I checked in with my Inner Guide, I knew I was making the right decision for me. Although I didn't need the external affirmation, I was pleased when speaking with a longtime friend, the next day. His response when I told him the news was, "That's the best thing I've heard all day!" He could see the potential in me and in my future. He wasn't worried, and neither was I.

In the next few months, I began to realize that as I shared my life-changing news with more people, their reactions had only to do with where they were coming from in their own lives: a place of fear or a place of excitement and adventure! They were either stuck in the confines of their Conditioned Self, one person going so far as to say that I was making a huge mistake that I would inevitably regret; or they were with me on my journey, full of encouragement and well wishes. Their reactions had nothing to do with me, but rather their own relationship to their world.

If others are not ready to hear you, then that is on them. You are not responsible for bringing them along. Don't let them pull you back to a lesser version of yourself. Soar. That is what you are meant to do. Allow that to happen. Catch yourself every time you feel the need to frame it or pull back or orchestrate any situation. Allow it to unfold. See where it goes. Play on the edges of what you were taught is appropriate. Watch the social conditioning in others – not to judge, but rather to know that you can no longer be bound by this restrictive policing of our human spirit. It is relentless and can mean the difference between a miserable life of barriers and restrictions that will only serve to choke you and your spirit to death, or lead you to a rich life of health and happiness; true bliss. Your choice.

CONTRACTION VS. EXPANSION

One of the most common limiting beliefs I notice people struggle with is Doubt. Doubt comes with Scarcity and is a manifestation of Conditioned Self. It is based on all the old stories we have been taught about ourselves and the world. We are not enough. I am not suggesting we ignore our Inner Knowing when something we are doing doesn't feel quite right, like when we get the sense that something or someone is not meant for us. That is not the same – that is important to attend to. For example, when you are deciding whether or not to take a job: check in with yourself. Notice the difference between when a direction you want to go gives you an expansive feeling or a contracted one. Listen to those messages.

If a direction or decision gives you an expanded feeling, and your mind or thoughts start to question everything about it, know that that is Conditioned Self providing you with a limiting belief that needs to be worked through. If you hear yourself thinking, "Oh, I can't do that!" or "That will never work!" or "What will they think of me if I do this?" Those are limiting beliefs, set in a Scarcity mindset.

Spiritual guide Michael Beckwith says, "We treat ourselves the way we were taught to think of ourselves." Most people, at some point in their lives, were given negative, limiting messages about themselves.

What messages do you hear? How do those messages impact how you treat yourself today? What do you need now to move from Scarcity to Abundance? What can you let go of to get beyond the doubt and the social conditioning that may be limiting your creativity and stopping you from receiving all that you deserve, keeping you from living your fullest life of meaning and joy?

MINDFULNESS PRACTICE 12
BREAKING FREE FROM DOUBT

Get comfortable in a seated position. Breathe. With your eyes closed or gazed down, focus on your inhales and exhales. Let go of any distractions that come into your awareness.

Continue to breathe deeply, and focus on your breath. Notice if your breath is soft and calm, or short and choppy. Notice where in your body you might be feeling any stress or tightness. See if, on your inhale, you can focus on that spot, and on your exhale, send some love and light into that area of your body. See if you can release even just a little bit of tension. Notice how it feels to let go.

Continue to breathe and with every breath, begin to relax just a little bit more. Consider your life so far and the direction it has gone. What feelings arise? Do you get a feeling of expansion in considering your life? Or a sense of contraction – a constriction in the chest or belly, perhaps? Or maybe a combination of both expansion and contraction?

Ask yourself: What keeps you (or might keep you) from fulfilling your life's purpose? What kind of social conditioning might be holding you back? Do you have a sense of doubt about moving forward? If so, what does the doubt that arises feel like? Where in your body do you experience doubt?

It might feel overwhelming. Doubt has had a whole lifetime of practice getting in your way. You may be witnessing it at this level for the first time. It's ok. You are not doubt. You are much bigger than that one emotion. You are simply witnessing your body experiencing doubt. It is the small voice that might be saying any version of: You can't do this! Who do you think you are? Don't be so rash! You'll fail!

This, or some version of this, may be a voice you are quite familiar with. It is the voice that believes, and wants you to believe, that you are not good enough. That you are simply not enough. Offer it compassion and gratitude. Conditioned

Self in the form of Doubt has done its job well: It has protected you from ventur-
ing off the beaten path you were taught you were supposed to stay on. Breathe
some fresh air into the area in your body where the doubt has gotten stuck.

Just know that this Conditioned Self has worked beautifully to stop you
from living an extraordinary life. It takes great courage to live the life you
want to live anyway, in spite of this voice. This is the moment when you get
to choose. Ordinary or extraordinary? It is your choice. This is your moment
to make a commitment to yourself to live an extraordinary life. To take your
life to the Next Level. Are you ready? What would it take for you to make that
leap? Sit with whatever comes up for you for a few minutes.

When you are ready, take a deep breath, and flutter your eyes open. Stretch
your body and take a moment to transition your focus back into the room.
Breathe.

Welcome back.

Feel free to journal now about your experience, or about any ideas or
insights that arose for you during this process.

Remember that doubt is tricky in that it can come back even when you
have done some work getting it unstuck. No worries; you can repeat this
mindfulness practice again and again, building the muscle that lessens the
potency and power of Conditioned Self over Inspired Self. The goal is not
to get rid of doubt forever, as it's questionable if that is even possible as a
human being. The level of your consciousness is measured by resiliency. It's a
matter of how quickly you can mindfully use the Observer to recognize your
challenges or limiting beliefs as they are, accept them, even welcome them
with an open heart, and when you (and they) are ready, to let them go.

How might you discover and clear away other limiting beliefs besides
doubt, that no longer serve you?

LIMITING BELIEFS INVENTORY

Start off by taking inventory of your limiting beliefs. Make a list of those
messages you have received and continue to believe about yourself that hold
you back. You can start off by asking what stops you from reaching your
potential and living your best life? The list may include items such as "I
can't…" or "I'm not good enough at…" This may take a few days. As each one
comes up, make note of it. Pay attention. These are the stumbling blocks that
can stop you from living the life of your dreams.

Once you have a list of limiting beliefs, one way to process them is through the work of best-selling author Byron Katie. In her book, *Loving What Is*, Katie invites us to challenge our thoughts and thought processes. She proposes four questions we can ask to lead us through that process, and I have added a fifth question. We can use the following mindfulness practice to challenge limiting beliefs.

MINDFULNESS PRACTICE 13
Challenging our Limiting Beliefs

Get comfortable in a seated position. Breathe. With your eyes closed or gazed down, focus on your inhales and exhales. Let go of any distractions that come into your awareness.

Consider a limiting belief from your inventory list, and ask yourself the following questions.

Question One: Is it true?

Perhaps based on your experience, or the stories you have been told about yourself, you believe it is, in fact, true.

Question Two: Can you absolutely know that it's true?

Using your Observer, consider whose idea this originally was. Consider the question: Says who? Is the assumption something that was told to you or said about you, and you believed it? Can you say that it is true beyond any doubt?

Question Three: How do you react? What happens when you believe that thought about yourself? What does it feel like in your body?

Does believing the thought give you an expansive, open-hearted feeling? or a closed, contracted feeling? How might this assumption be affecting your sense of self, of who you really are? Might it be covering up your Inspired Self?

Question Four: Who would you be without the thought?

What might your life/thoughts/actions be without this assumption? What might it feel like in your body to be liberated from this long-held misconception? Stay with that feeling as long as you like – even get used to it! When we let go of an idea that no longer serves us, it is often useful to replace it with something useful – perhaps a new idea or positive affirmation. I like to add:

Question Five: What thought or idea could you call to mind to replace your now debunked assumption? What might a different thought be that would affirm all that you are?

Consider something positive like, "I have so much potential," or "I believe in me," or as my friend likes to say, "I love me some me."

Make a pact with yourself that the next time you notice a limiting belief arise, you will focus on your response to my fifth question.

When you are ready, take another deep breath, and flutter your eyes open. Stretch your body and take a moment to transition your focus back into the room.

Welcome back.

Feel free to journal now about your experience, or about any ideas or insights that arose for you.

Letting go of what no longer serves us can feel like true freedom. And sometimes, the letting go process can take the form of tears or grief of losing what we have been holding onto so tightly, even if it is difficult or challenging. Or it could take the form of frustration that we've been holding onto these notions about ourselves for so long, and wished we could have let them go sooner. How we see ourselves and our lives can be transformed forever with these practices. What is waiting to emerge beyond our limiting beliefs? Does that question bring about excitement? Wonder? More fear or doubt? Sit with whatever comes up for you.

Maintain expanded awareness and a sense of love rather than fear, as often as possible. We can check in with our deep Inner Knowing and connect to our higher purpose – what we are called or have chosen to do. We can let go of other people's perceptions and limiting restrictions of Conditioned Self, and know we will be heard and seen, and experience a joy that is unsurpassed.

MANIPULATORS VS. MAGNETS

Before my life was disrupted by the harsh awareness of my childhood trauma, I was in a constant frenzy; my days were made up of to-do lists that usually got longer throughout the day rather than shorter. Yet I was extremely effective at accomplishing my tasks. I got more done in a day than most people get done in a week. And if you recognize yourself in this description, have no fear, there is no judgment here. I know that when I was living in this way, however, I was pushing myself so hard; I believed that achieving tasks meant achieving happiness. I never really stopped to enjoy anything I had accomplished during my day, so that elusive happiness was always one unfinished task out of my reach. In fact, on those rare occasions that I did complete my overflowing to-do list in the allotted timeframe, I still didn't enjoy the achievement; I would immediately try to get a head start on the next day's list. What a grind I was living – of my own volition! Push, push, push.

When we are rooted in Scarcity, fear, lack, never enough, and an intense drive to succeed, we are living from our Conditioned Self, and as what I like to refer to as a "Manipulator." Manipulators are focused first and foremost on the outcome. They believe if they just work hard enough, longer hours, and pound the pavement, then they will rattle up enough business to thrive. And if they get lucky, they might find that elusive success they always dreamed of. Manipulators are constantly pushing themselves to do more; there is a sense that they must prove themselves. Manipulators often go through life in a whirlwind, and often do get a lot done; They might find "success," but at the expense of their own happiness, life, health, and loved ones.

On the other hand, Abundance breeds Magnets – those who have done their work, discovered their higher purpose, set their intentions, asked for what they desire, and set up the circumstances to bring about all the opportunities. While Manipulators focus on the How: how do I get done as much as humanly possible in one day, often from a place of distrust and scarcity; Magnets focus on the Why: Why am I here? What is my higher purpose? Magnets are drawn to opportunities that manifest their higher purpose, and those prospects are drawn to them. There is an energetic resonance that brings those opportunities in: a *pull* rather than a *push*.

If you have ever done something and afterwards thought, "I'm not sure why I went down that path, but I felt drawn to do so, and it felt right to do so." This is your Magnet self – its energy can be subtle or extremely insistent, but it often takes a willingness to listen to your Inspired Self and the trust to follow those intuitive senses – even when they go against what you have been conditioned to believe you are "supposed" to do.

This is not to say that Magnets are not achievers, or that they sit around and do nothing all day and just expect their dreams to manifest. Magnets get still and follow the guidance of their Inspired Self to move forward. They follow what gives them a feeling of expansion rather what makes them feel contracted. And the smallest step they take in that direction of expansion is often met by an abundance of opportunities, filled with promise, hope, and joy.

My Midwest realtor coaching client, Danita, had done her work. When she called me, she was in Manipulator mode, feeling trapped by circumstances, and living in fear, uncertainty, and scarcity. She had simply stepped out of alignment – which we all do from time to time. I reminded her of all the work she had already done acknowledging and clearing away her limiting beliefs, and then I assured her that success was only a breath away – on the other side of a paper-thin veil of resistance. This resistance came in the form of an unwillingness to receive. All she had to do was to blow the paper away, and practice receiving. I offered her a mantra: "I am worthy of success, and it is on its way to me." I told her to trust that it is coming! That I sensed that she had already run the proverbial marathon – doing the work of letting go of limiting beliefs, and that she was just about to take her victory lap! She told me it was exactly what she was longing to hear.

WILLINGNESS TO RECEIVE

Once we have gained some clarity around what stops us from living our most meaningful life, and have processed some of those roadblocks, we also must be willing to receive the gifts we have asked for. Based on our life's experiences and social identities, we may be more used to accepting and expecting gifts. This is where the notion of privilege and unearned entitlement comes in. We all have some form of privilege, and so have likely been taught in some way to expect people around us to behave in certain ways that validate or include us, whether we have acknowledged that or not. As a white person, I have been taught to expect trust from those around me. If you are male, you may have been taught to assume people will believe you when you speak. This is not something women, especially women of color can reasonably assume. Some of us have learned to expect fair treatment while others, from a lifetime of daily invalidations, have experienced the opposite. As we consider cultivating a willingness to receive divine gifts or opportunities that become available to us, it is important to note that we are not all starting from the same vantage point.

That said, many of us are taught we are not good enough and so for one reason or another do not deserve these opportunities or to have our deepest desires materialize. I believe this is what was stopping Danita. Having lived a life marked by physical and emotional struggles, she had little experience receiving gifts. She had no point of reference.

For some of us, it is a practice to learn to receive. This is why so many of the mindfulness practices in this book invite you to sit in the feeling of Inspiration. We don't hang out in this feeling very often, certainly not enough. This is a place where we can dream big and practice feeling what it feels like to already be a success, to feel love, to feel cared for. What if we thought of this place of Inspiration, this expanded awareness, as our Home: our starting place?

What if you chose to spend some time in this space during your meditation every single day? How might that change the way you live? The way you interact with others? Might it change the path of your life?

A YES! MENTALITY – LIVING IN THE FLOW

Having lived a life rooted mostly in fear, doubt, and Scarcity, the shift I made toward Abundance included noticing signs of opportunities in my life that had begun to show up, and to see them as manifestations of what I had asked the Universe for in my intention-setting meditations. I made the choice to receive those gifts and opportunities, and began to live with a Yes! mentality. I began to see how I was living in the Flow and how I was living in Abundance, rather than in Scarcity. And the more I was able to recognize the Flow and point out specific opportunities that began to show up in my life, the more my desires seemed to emerge. Remember, where our focus goes, energy flows. I let go of grasping for what I did not yet have, and began to revel in what I am already surrounded by: a wondrous life, friends and family who constantly bestow love on me, a new direction in my career that allows me to serve in ways I never before dreamed, and many other gifts.

As my life began to manifest more, I was most surprised by how my capacity for expansion increased. In other words, the more I opened to possibilities, the more I was able to receive. It was truly miraculous. I noticed this not only in how wide my spectrum of sight became in my meditation (to the stratosphere!), but also when I would respond to a friend's simple question of "what's new?" and it would take me half an hour to share all that was new. I often surprised myself by my answers. I was not trying to boast, but rather to share my life. More often than not, my friends would comment on the excitement in my eyes, the glowing expression on my face as I talked about what's new!

I am reminded of the oft quoted sentiment by Marianne Williamson, "Our deepest fear is not that we are inadequate. Our deepest fear is that we are powerful beyond measure. It is our light, not our darkness that most frightens us."

What would your life be like if you were able to truly embrace your light? Here is what the process can look like:

1. Set intentions for what you would like to manifest.
2. Discover what stops you (your limiting beliefs).
3. Clear the path by letting go of what no longer serves you.
4. Be open to receiving by knowing that you are enough and that you deserve and are worthy to receive what you ask for.
5. Allow it to arrive with openheartedness, abundance, patience, joy, and Gratitude.

I choose to embrace my light with humility and gratitude for all that I have been given, and all the opportunities that emerge that allow me to share that light, and be of service to others. And so can you. Gratitude is a wonderful tool in this process of expanding your life, and taking it to the next level (more on this topic in the next chapter). When you start off each day in gratitude for what you already have, you become even more grateful for what comes your way.

CHAPTER 8

Going Deeper:
Mindfully Staying on Track

"Life's challenges are not supposed to paralyze you;
they're supposed to help you discover who you are."
~Bernice Johnson Reagon

"Promise me you'll always remember: You're braver than you believe, and
stronger than you seem, and smarter than you think."
~Christopher Robin to Pooh, A.A. Milne

"I just want to be happy!" This is a very common refrain when people
are asked what they want out of life. And through mindfulness practices,
we can actually cultivate that happiness. It might be easy to maintain our
intentions and our cultivated joy while in meditation or even on a retreat.
What happens, however, when we are confronted with the challenges that
inevitably come with living on this planet? When we open our eyes, or come
out of meditation, sometimes we are bombarded by horrific news or negative
energy. We seamlessly forget who we really are and the peaceful meditation
or rest we just emerged from, and are catapulted into our age-old patterns of
irritation and disturbance. We become vestiges of our stories, or we create
stories about what is happening – all behaviors that go against our purpose,
intention, and the joy that we have just cultivated. What do we do? How do
we get our sense of peace back?

Before gathering specific strategies that we can use in these challenging
moments, let's think about what is happening subconsciously, beneath the

surface. In the midst of whatever we are currently experiencing, has who we really are changed at all? No. But the perception of our situation may have shifted, or sunken to a lower energy level. We might even say in these moments, "It's not fair! I just want to be happy!" But is that really true?

Author of *Start Where You Are*, Chris Gardner recommends the following activity, which I recently invited my students in one of my mindfulness courses to try. They were stunned by their results. All you'll need is two blank, unlined pieces of paper (8.5 x 11 or larger), and a marker.

GARDNER'S LIFE MAPPING

Take a moment to consider your life so far. Its ups and downs.

Now take one of the sheets of paper, and place it down horizontally, so the long edge is in front of you. The long edge will represent time. The shorter edge represents your level of happiness.

Start your pen at the very left edge of the paper, representing your birth time, however high or low on the paper you might consider your happiness with life. With your life's journey in mind, from that birth time as your starting point, draw a line across the page representing the peaks and valleys you have experienced up until now. *Now* would be the right edge of the paper.

When you have completed your line, take a moment to reflect on your drawing. What were the circumstances that surrounded your lowest points? What were the circumstances that surrounded your highest points? Were you living from Inspired Self or Conditioned Self at each of these points? What were your biggest times of learning and growth? Reflect on these questions for a while, and feel free to journal about whatever insights these questions prompt in you.

Now move that piece of paper aside, and place the other piece of paper in front of you, horizontally again. Once again, the long edge represents time; the short edge represents your level of happiness. This time, however, the left edge of the paper signifies now, and the right edge signifies the future, perhaps to your physical death or transition. Start from the left side of the paper, the *now*, however high or low you might consider your current level of happiness with life. From that starting point, draw a line representing how you would like your life to go with regards to your happiness.

When you're done, take a moment to reflect on this drawing. Is it a straight line? If it's not, are there big dips, or small ones? Are you surprised by what you drew?

My students were stunned that their drawings were not straight lines at the top of the page. Not a single one had drawn a straight line. Although their lines were all in the upper half of their paper, they had still drawn peaks and valleys. It was clear that although they were definitely interested in their own happiness, they also valued the learning and growth that comes with the challenges life brings. Interestingly, in her global research, psychology professor, Jeanne Tsai found that everyone wants to be happy, but what that looks like can be culturally determined. She found that whereas white American students want to be excited and entertained, Chinese students want to be peaceful, and Asian Americans fell somewhere in between. What happiness looks like maybe different from one culture to the next, but *that* we want to be happy is universal.

If happiness is a worldwide goal, and yet we expect and even desire some dips in our drawing, how can we reframe our challenging moments, mindfully implement our Observer, and know that whatever we are experiencing, as difficult as it is, may just be a blip or a valley on our path forward? Sometimes that process is easier said than done, I realize.

WHEN WE GET STUCK

Have you ever had one of those days where it's a calamity of errors? It feels like the Universe is conspiring against just you. I had one of those days recently. I got up later than I had intended to, and after my peaceful meditation, I got a text message on my phone saying a dear friend's health was at risk again. As my anxiety began to build, I rushed through my workout so I would be on time to my first meeting of the day with a potential client. Not realizing it had snowed overnight, I hadn't left time to de-ice my windshield and so did so as quickly as I could. As I was driving to my meeting, I hit every single red light. I tried to use those extra minutes for some deep breathing, and although it helped, I could feel that I was still tense. I got to my meeting with no time to spare only to find it had been rescheduled!

We have all had those days. This is when our head starts reeling and we start re-thinking our purpose in life and questioning whether we are on the right track, or if the Universe was really trying to tell us something that maybe we should just go back home, climb into bed and give up!

THAT DANG RABBIT HOLE!

On days like this when it is extra challenging to stay connected to my Inspired Self, I know that I have plunged headfirst into what I refer to as

The Rabbit Hole. This is the place where all we can see is darkness. Ego/ Conditioned Self has completely taken over and our thinking mind relives all the old ways we have thought about ourselves and our lives. Doubt and fear become the air we breathe, and we are paralyzed to move forward. We start rethinking every decision we have ever made and start listening to the critic in our minds that tells us we are incompetent, insufficient, and basically useless. What we are conditioned to do at this point is to drop even deeper down into the hole. As we tell ourselves we are not enough, we begin to believe it and things just keep getting worse from there. (Where our focus goes, energy grows.) You've been there, right?

So, what do we do when we are stuck in this rabbit hole? The very first thing we can do is remarkably simple: Just look up! As soon as we actually remember to look up, we see the light and recognize that we are, in fact, in the rabbit hole. If you don't recognize the situation as a rabbit hole, on the other hand, you can stay stuck in there thinking that that is the only possible reality. This mindfulness practice of looking up and acknowledging the rabbit hole is sometimes enough to bring about a shift in perception and consequently, some relief. When you look up, your reality shifts and you see not just the light, but a way out.

Using the Observer, looking up reminds us, too, who we really are, and that whatever challenges we are facing in this moment, have nothing to do with our Inspired Self or our expanded, conscious awareness. Who we really are has not changed at all. What we are experiencing in the rabbit hole are just challenges that this body is undergoing in this moment. These challenges are usually brought about by Conditioned Self trying to control the way things go, or wishing things were different than they are, or some other manifestation that makes us feel anxious and contracted. Once we connect to who we really are, and remember that we are much bigger than the skin we are in – and that we are not our problems, our stories, or what anyone else says about us – we begin to realize that we have choices. We don't have to stay stuck in the rabbit hole, we can choose to get out. Physical movement is a great option for this. Get some fresh air and do any kind of exercise, if at all possible.

You can also contact a friend who, as Brené Brown suggests, has earned the right to hear your story: someone who has your back, and will be a sense of support for you. Sometimes laughing with a friend is the best way to leap out of the hole. During my worst days of suffering, I would call one of my closest friends who would metaphorically lower a rope, and let me know I wasn't alone down there. She taught me that whatever I was experiencing, whatever situation I was in, was temporary. I would share with her some horrible feeling or situation I felt stuck in, and she would add the words, "for now..." which offered me perspective and reminded me that this too shall pass. Sitting with me, even over the phone, alleviated my sense of impending doom that the rabbit hole brings, and also provided me with a sense of relief, connection, and light. Now, when I am upset or bothered about something and I reach out to her, all she has to say is, "Might you be down a rabbit hole?" and those words immediately bring recognition and perspective. Ah, I didn't recognize that is where I was! I see it now. I know what to do.

GETTING GROUNDED

When you feel disconnected or misaligned, another excellent tool for finding your alignment with your Inspired Self is engaging in a grounding mindfulness practice. This can be helpful anytime you start to feel anxious about the past or the future. We often get stressed when we perceive that things aren't going the way we want them to, or the way we had planned, or expected them to go. Grounding helps you focus on the present moment and let go of any attachment to the outcome. It also serves as a temporary antidote to dealing with trauma or post-traumatic stress, in this moment. For longer-term and deeper healing, meeting with a therapist is required. Even if you have tried talk therapy before and you felt like it was ineffective, finding a counselor who you feel a connection with, and coming to therapy from a place of mindfulness, can bring about profound movement in your journey.

MINDFULNESS PRACTICE 14
Root to Rise

Get comfortable in a seated position. Breathe. With your eyes closed or gazed down, focus on your inhales and exhales. Let go of any distractions that come into your awareness.

Notice your body in your seat. Focus on your feet. As you feel your feet on the ground, know that the earth contains energy and strength that supports us always.

Now imagine that your body is a tree. Imagine your feet are the tree's roots. As you breathe in, imagine your feet drawing in the energy and strength from the earth as if it were soaking up water on a hot day. With each breath in, take big gulps of air to facilitate the movement of energy up into your feet. As you exhale, breathe out any tension or anxiety that is stored in your body.

On your next inhale, allow the energy from the earth to make its way all the way up your legs toward your spinal column. Again, exhale any tension in your body. Inhale, allow the energy to rise along your spine, stopping along the way to provide strength to whatever part of your body needs it: your pelvis, your solar plexus, your heart, your throat, between your eyes. Allow yourself to rest in that strength for as many breaths as you like.

As the energy from the earth makes its way up to the top of your head, exhale and allow the energy to free itself from your body like a geyser, releasing into the air above you and beyond. Imagine you are a spark and the energy is fireworks. As it is released from your body, it rises high and floats down into arcs all around you, as though you are encompassed by positivity and strength. Inhale that energy in the electric air you have created around you. And find stillness in that space.

As you focus now on your feet again, notice if they feel heavier, more connected to the earth. As you root them into the ground by pressing them down, notice that your spine can straighten up a little more, making you just a little taller. In yoga practice, we call this, Root to Rise. The more you root down and feel grounded, the higher you can ascend, the more expansive you feel, ready for anything!

When you're ready, take another deep breath, and flutter your eyes open. Stretch your body and take a moment to transition your focus back into the room.

Welcome back.

Feel free to journal now about your experience, or about any ideas or insights that arose for you.

Grounding is a useful tool that you can access at any time during the day. As soon as you feel off-track or ready to snap, you can simply focus on your feet on the ground and remember who you really are. Root to rise. I actually prefer thinking of it this way: Root to Soar!

MORE STRATEGIES FOR GETTING UNSTUCK

My friend Debbie reminded me recently to "Celebrate the mess you're in!" What if we could welcome the challenges, brought about and often exacerbated by Conditioned Self, as opportunities for growth and learning?

This can be extremely difficult to do. It is a practice, but provides a way out of intense suffering. The following are some other mindfulness practices that can serve as strategies for minimizing distress.

Michael Beckwith suggests that when we fall out of alignment, we sometimes fall into lower level thinking. We start to lose our trust that the Universe has our backs and we end up asking self-defeating questions. Rather than asking "Why me?" or "What am I supposed to do now?", he suggests we consider asking higher level questions that remind us who we really are, and raise our energy up such as, "What is my higher purpose?" Or we can remember to ask ourselves, "Oh yeah, before this challenge or disturbance seemed to get in my way, I was on the path to fulfilling my life's purpose. What would it take to put me back on that path?"

I have had many opportunities to use this technique and have found relief in doing so. Not too long ago, I was struggling from a rejection of a potential consulting gig, and I started to spiral into the rabbit hole. All kinds of thoughts came up like, "You can't do this, and you're not good enough, and what makes you think you can succeed, blah blah blah." I was sliding down the rabbit hole, picking up speed. But before too long, I remembered to use my mindfulness practice of looking up, connecting with my Inspired Self, and I asked myself Beckwith's question, "What is needed right now to put me back on my path?" The answer came quickly from within. My Inspired Self whispered, "Trust." And I instantly felt better because I realized that this was just a dip in the road on my Life Map, and that I could absolutely trust that the Universe has my back and will offer many more opportunities.

Soon after that, I was inspired by author and life coach, Tama Kieves, who suggests that when we get rejected or get a "No" when we desperately hoped for a "Yes!" that we stop rehashing the old story of loss and deprivation. Instead, she recommends that we ask the question, "What opportunity am I being given in this moment?" If we persist in perceiving what's happening to us as a loss, at least ask the question, "OK, if something is being taken away so we can experience something else; what is that something else?" Asking this question is a higher energy question and can help lift us out of the rabbit hole, but only if we remember, and are willing, to ask it. Oprah has said, "Your losses are there to wake you up – to put you back on course of your life's purpose."

And if we truly make the conscious choice to believe that the Universe has our back, and is conspiring on our behalf, then when we get a rejection or our expectations are met with what we perceive as a resounding denial of our wishes, consider that perhaps the Universe has something much bigger and better in store for you. You might even find some gratitude for avoiding a path that might have been much narrower or more limited than what the Universe has in store. Another mark of one's level of conscious awakening is how gracefully we are able to let go of what was never meant for us.

A great mindfulness practice is: as you inhale, feel your body open to receiving what is waiting to emerge. As you exhale, let go of what no longer serves you. Repeating this process several times can move you forward when you are feeling stuck.

MINDFUL DECISION-MAKING

While it may not be easy to change our behavior, in her best-selling book *The 5 Second Rule*, Mel Robbins says that it can be easier than we think. She says that when we have what she calls an impulse from our Inner Knowing (not a contracted feeling from Conditioned Self as in, for example, an impulse purchase, but rather a deep, expansive knowing), within five seconds, our brain/thoughts begin to magnify the risk of taking action on that impulse, and we hesitate. We get overwhelmed with reasons not to do it, and we reject the impulse, and with it, our chance to change our lives.

Robbins proposes we can change that hesitation into action. Her solution is the 5-Second Rule: that as we notice the whisper of our Inner Knowing, we can immediately start counting backwards from 5. When we reach "1," start moving, writing, talking, or whatever will move you in the direction of your life goals and intentions. This also works when we are stuck in the rut of a bad habit. As soon as we notice that we are about to engage in the bad habit, we have 5 seconds to change our behavior, and in effect, change our lives.

Although Robbins does not frame it this way, her 5-Second Rule is a mindfulness practice because it requires that we notice our thoughts in the moment and how they stop us from living our best life. Mindful awareness of our thoughts and actions allows us to pause, count from 5 to 1 and choose to act, rather than proceeding mindlessly through life. We can take action before our social conditioning has a chance to step in and stop us. Life comes down to decisions – change your actions and you change your life.

When you are trying to make a potentially life-altering decision, consider whether you are going in a direction toward grief or relief. For example, it was clear to me that when I thought about leaving the university after almost twenty years, I felt an overwhelming sense of relief, and although I will miss teaching in the classroom, and my colleagues, the relief is much stronger than the grief of leaving. If the sense of grief was stronger than the relief, that would indicate that perhaps it was too soon to leave. This strategy can be useful when you are struggling with a tough decision.

Going back to the notion of expansion versus contraction is also useful in decision-making. Notice what happens in your body when you think about making a specific decision. Does it make you feel contracted in your body, or expansive? What about if you made a different decision? How does that sit with you? Which decision are you intuitively drawn towards? That is usually the direction that your Inner Knowing is guiding you to go, and will be more likely to put you in alignment with your higher purpose, even if you can see potential roadblocks along the way.

Of course, we all have to make choices sometimes that are not necessarily what we are drawn toward, such as going to the doctor or caring for someone who is sick (unless either of those bring you a feeling of happiness). In these cases, fulfill the obligation as quickly, efficiently, and compassionately (even to yourself) as possible, and move on, feeling the satisfaction of a job well done.

Yoga specialist Baron Baptiste reminds us to "Try Easy." If we feel like we are struggling, or forcing something, whether it be in a yoga posture on the mat, or in our mind or experience off the mat, he suggests we notice the struggle and see what we can let go of, or soften. In other words, it is our resistance to the situation that is causing our suffering. If we can soften to the experience (in our body or in our life), then we are more likely to not only move through it, but also to go much farther down our path than we would have otherwise. If life is happening *for* us and not *to* us, then there really is no need to fight life anyway. Allow it to unfold, and consider trusting that it will do so in the best way for you.

GRATITUDE

It is difficult, if not impossible, to be grateful and be in scarcity mode at the same time. They are simply contradictory. Gratitude allows us to take in all that we are in the present moment, and offer up thanks. Gratitude can create expansion; whereas scarcity creates contraction.

The gratitude mindfulness practice below helped me out of an extremely challenging time when I was traveling in Israel with my family. I was still in recovery mode from dealing with my childhood trauma and in a moment of impatience with how long the process was taking, decided to plan an incredible family trip for the following summer. I think I assumed at some point a timer would ding between then and that next summer and ta-da, I would be completely healed! Hah!

I bought non-refundable tickets and when the time arrived, off we went. After spending one of our days in record-high heat of 125 degrees, I was physically drained, and the stress of travel in another country started to wear on me. We were on a bus in the middle of the country, and I felt the walls of the bus begin to close in on me. I was beginning to panic. My heart started to beat out of my chest, my stomach began to churn, and I thought I would pass out.

Suddenly, mercifully, I remembered my practice. I started to breathe deeply and practiced mindful grounding. I focused on how my feet felt touching the floor of the bus. This definitely helped, but it wasn't until I began to find gratitude that the real transformation happened. I focused on the present moment. I noticed all that was good in this moment: I was no longer in the sweltering heat, but felt gratitude that I was instead in an air-conditioned bus. My body felt cool even. I was no longer standing on my feet, but felt gratitude that I had been graciously given a comfortable seat. My feet were given a reprieve. As this practice continued, I breathed easier. I could feel the air in my lungs – inhaling and exhaling. I was grateful for the ability to breathe normally. And once I was able to focus beyond my own body, I was grateful for the fact that I had my family sitting next to me. I was not alone, and I knew they were willing and able to support or assist me if I needed it. I could finally start to just be grateful for the privilege of being together on such an incredible trip. Where our focus goes, energy flows. And so, within minutes, with mindful gratitude, I went from panic to appreciation, from complete contraction to outright expansion.

MINDFULNESS PRACTICE 15
Finding Gratitude

Get comfortable in a seated position. Breathe. With your eyes closed or gazed down, focus on your inhales and exhales. Let go of any distractions that come into your awareness.

As you inhale, notice any place in your body that feels contracted in any way. Notice any nervous tension or energy inside you. As you exhale, breathe love and light into those spaces. See if you can soften them at all.

If it is available to you, open your arms wide so that you can open your heart. Breathe deeply.

When you are ready, bring your hands together either in your lap, or if it feels appropriate, and is available to you, bring them to heart center, palm to palm, thumbs gently pressed into your chest. When your hands meet, you are closing the circuit that brings loving, expanded energy from your heart through your arms to your hands. Breathe deeply imagining that energy expanding out from your heart.

Now, consider one thing you are grateful for. Even ask yourself: What am I grateful for? It could be your life, your body, or even your breath. Focus on your breath again. Inhale gratitude, and on your exhale, send compassion to yourself for finding something to be grateful for in this moment.

If you can think of another thing to give thanks for, do so, and continue the breathing pattern. If possible, come up with at least three things to be grateful for as you breathe in gratitude for each one and exhale compassion and kindness to yourself. Continue this pattern for as long as you like. See if it doesn't make the edges of your mouth raise up just a little!

When you are ready, take another deep breath, and flutter your eyes open. Stretch your body and take a moment to transition your focus back into the room.

Welcome back.

Feel free to journal now about your experience, or about any ideas or insights that arose for you.

This practice can be a daily habit to start or end any other meditation, or it can be used whenever you start feeling stressed or out of alignment. It puts you into a state of Abundance. What a great way to start the day!

Finding gratitude is a great tool for getting unstuck as soon as stuckness occurs. I will say, however, that it is not always available. When I was dealing with my own trauma, I sometimes had a very difficult time finding gratitude. When I was in the thick of suffering, I remember thinking, I know if I can find something to be grateful for, it would help, but I could not do it. I was so caught up in the horror and unfairness of what I was experiencing remembering my tortured childhood that gratitude was not even an option. It felt inauthentic to even try.

To allow challenging feelings to surface, and to sit with them can be healing; however, when we feel stuck in them, and feel like we cannot move forward, we can mindfully consider: what might make me feel just a little bit better in this moment? What would make me feel just a little more expansive? As Oprah has also been known to say, "Your job is to figure out, what is the next right move? You don't need to know all the moves, just the next right move." Once I listened for the answer and knew what to do, I opened up to a slightly more expansive mode and then I was able to move into a practice of gratitude, which allowed my expansiveness to grow.

HONORING OURSELVES

Social conditioning makes staying on track when we get stuck exceedingly difficult. Even if you had a wonderful childhood, chances are that somewhere along the line you had an experience that made you feel you were not good enough. As these messages seep into our thoughts, they create self-loathing. And this cycle is yet another way we can get stuck. Consider listening to the messages you tell yourself throughout your day. Are they positive or negative? Are you as supportive as you would be to a close friend? If not, how might these messages be stopping you from loving yourself? If we don't love ourselves, how can we expect others to love us?

Most teachers have an underlying message that they hope to convey to their students. Yoga instructors are no different. One of the key concepts I bring to every class is this: What if we are perfect just as we are? Take a moment to sit with this idea. Your Conditioned Self may be screaming at me, "Heck no, I have so much more work to do!"

We can always empower ourselves further, and of course we have plenty of growth and learning ahead of us. But what if we already have all that we need to live our best possible life? Rather than striving toward perfection, what if we immersed ourselves in the Perfection that we already are? It is a whole different way of moving forward. Rather than perceiving ourselves from a place of Scarcity, we can instead move forward from a place of Abundance.

I always say to yoga practitioners, yoga begins when we honor our bodies just as they are in this moment. On the mat that might mean taking it easy today rather than pushing. Or perhaps you have extra energy today, and honoring your body means seeing what it can do! It all comes back to what makes us feel expanded or contracted, both on the mat and off it, in any given moment, on any given day. Honoring ourselves means mindfully giving ourselves compassion and love, letting go of self-judgment, no matter where we are, or even, when we make what we have been trained to believe are "mistakes."

At the tender age of four, I attempted to pick up a gallon of milk to pour myself a glass at the dinner table. I remember the empowered feelings both of wanting to do it myself and not having to ask for help. I was daring myself into action and I was nervous and excited by the possibility.

The milk container probably weighed half as much as I did, and it took all of my strength to lift it. You can imagine where this is going! As the spout of the milk container came in contact with the glass and I started to pour, the glass tipped over and the milk from the container went everywhere, and I mean everywhere!

The resulting mayhem that ensued at the kitchen table and the vitriol that was directed at me in that moment was so intense and made me so uncomfortable and afraid that I remember thinking at that young age, "Wow, I must be an idiot for trying that! I'll never do that again!"

I did not cry over the spilled milk, but the underlying message was very clear: Mistakes are to be avoided at all costs.

That was the beginning of my socialization into that message. And looking back, it is clear that this is what our society teaches us. We are so afraid of making a mistake and being misunderstood, yelled at, or worse, being ostracized, we learn to force ourselves into someone else's idea of what we should or should not do. Conditioned Self trains us to maintain the status quo, stifle our curiosity and creativity, so we do not venture outside the box and make others or ourselves uncomfortable. Ever.

One of my clients told me he was taught at an early age to always consider his actions so that he would never make the same mistake twice. Mark grew up consumed with this rule; believing there is always a right and wrong way to do things, and living in fear of doing it wrong, or less than optimally. His hypervigilance caused him stress and anxiety, and it was all based on a story he was taught – that mistakes are to be avoided at all costs.

What if making mistakes could be reframed? What if instead of being afraid of being or doing something wrong, we chose instead to claim our mistakes as learning opportunities? Yes! I took a risk and lost. That does not mean I should never take a risk again, but it does mean that I am willing to live large. Reframing mistakes allows us the freedom to engage, to grow, to be creative, to show up fully, and as Brené Brown suggests in her book *Daring Greatly*, to step into the arena rather than staying on the sidelines. Consider how much richer our lives would be if we were inclined to take such risks! Obviously, if we hurt someone from something we say or do, we must apologize, but sometimes those apologies, if handled well (see next chapter), can ultimately build a deeper relationship.

Ultimately, when we get stuck, focusing on the present moment and listening to our Inspired Self helps us to get back in alignment with our highest purpose. The mindfulness practices offered so far have focused on empowering us to live our best life. Essentially, these practices can guide us to connect deeply within ourselves and listen to our life's calling. We can soar by ourselves, but we do not live in a vacuum.

As humans, we are social creatures. We have an inherent need to connect with others. As it turns out, the mindfulness practices in this book that we can implement to connect with and stay in alignment with our Inspired Self, are the exact same practices we need to connect with others to find meaning and belonging. They are the perfect preparation for living beyond our social conditioning to create deep, authentic relationships that we never imagined possible. Our practice is to ask: How can we use what we have learned to build significant, fulfilling, supportive, loving relationships, and with whom?

CHAPTER 9

What Stops Us from Building Relationships Across Difference

To overcome our biases, we must walk boldly towards them.
~Verne Myers

A few years back, I was attending a workshop led by my dear friend and colleague, Dr. Stephany Rose. She asked us to sit in pairs with someone we did not know and preferably someone whose race was different from our own. We were invited to sit directly across from this person, knees to knees, and stare into each other's eyes for four minutes. She cited research that found that doing so could completely alter the way we interact with another human being. This, she said, was one way of transcending our perceived differences.

Four minutes is a long time to stare into the eyes of someone you love, let alone someone you haven't even met yet. But I must say I did notice a shift in my perception over the course of the four minutes. At the beginning, I found myself making all kinds of assumptions about the person in front of me. I imagined where she grew up, the kind of life she might have lived, and what her life must have been like up until that point. However, as I mindfully noticed the thoughts that were coming up, I began to let them go. And I immediately began to see the humanity in her eyes. I started to see how looking at her was like looking into a mirror – not because we looked anything alike, but because I could see and deeply sense our common humanity. I felt both the joy and the pain we might each have experienced in our respective lives. It wasn't the same joy or pain, but rather a shared understanding that life brings us all joy and pain. When the four minutes were up, we smiled at each other and I could feel a deep sense of connection.

This was a profound experience for me. I kept wondering what it would be like if we could do this exercise with one other person every day – how we would start to connect with each other differently in the world. If we could see each other as human, not as though we are the same, but as sacred, it might transform our interactions. When we connect deeply with other human beings, our social conditioning takes a back seat, and we are free to be ourselves.

But social conditioning prohibits us from deeply connecting with each other, especially across social differences. So we are left segregated from each other, interacting as often as possible only with people who look like ourselves or whose social identities match our own. And it goes deeper than this. There is a system in place that makes it so that we will stay segregated. The more we remain separate, the less empowered we are to actually create change at the systemic level. Without change, the system continues to empower those in power, to stay in power. Our freedom, health, and wellbeing are at risk here if we continue on the current path.

Because of the system of inequality that informs all of our lives, we live in a segregated, isolated world where we have a lack of social belongingness – one of Maslow's primary needs in his pyramid. In order to understand how this system operates in our lives, I have often invited students and workshop participants to engage in the following activity. It asks them to acknowledge their socialization: how they know or have learned what they know or believe to be true. Or in other words, to consider the impact that learned biases and behavior have on their own thought processes.

ACKNOWLEDGING YOUR SOCIALIZATION

When we meet someone for the first time, or see someone we don't know walking towards us, our minds have been trained to focus on certain aspects of them. We might focus on their perceived social class, race, or gender, etc. What stands out to us is often what we have been taught to focus on, but not discuss.

The next time you are being introduced to a person for the first time or see a person whom you don't know walk towards you, be aware of what you focus on in this situation. (This is before you meet them, before they speak or interact with you.) Based on their perceived social group memberships, what thoughts come to mind as you are being introduced? Mindfully notice:

- What are your assumptions about this specific person?
- What feelings/emotions arise as you make these assumptions?
- Are these assumptions based on your own past experiences or on stereotypes you have been taught to believe?
- How might these assumptions turn into barriers to interaction with this person?
- What might be some other consequences of making these assumptions?
- How does our socialization about social identities work to make us want to include some people, and make us want to exclude others?
- Reflect on this experience. What did you learn about yourself?

My students and participants are often appalled by what this activity brings up for them. They often say that before doing this exercise, they thought they didn't buy into stereotypes, but when they were asked to mindfully focus on their own thoughts about a person they didn't know, all kinds of stereotypes arose.

I make sure they know that this assignment is not meant to shame or blame them for their thoughts, but rather to notice how biases and stereotypes have, through osmosis, seeped into their mind. I think about it like this. Imagine you are at the base of a waterfall, say Niagra Falls, and the water represents all of the 5,000 media ads we take in every day – many of them full of biases and stereotypes. How can we not be affected by these messages?

Our work is to acknowledge that we are under the waterfall and that in order to challenge those biases, we must take a good look at the water crashing down and allow it to fall around you. Notice how it impacts you; notice how it impacts others. Notice the power of our socialization and how we are taught and expected to simply marinate in all the messages.

Until we know these biases are in our head, we cannot do anything to change them. The result is that we live in a state of fear and mistrust of people whose social identities are different than our own, well-grounded by past experience or not. Or worse, we actually believe the stereotypes and misinformation we have been taught about groups of people, including the groups to which we belong.

THE POWER OF BELONGINGNESS

We live in a world that has a substantial legacy of domination and systemic inequality that undergirds all of our daily lives (arguably our economic system, political system, legal system, among others). Although none of us who are alive today created that system, we are a part of it by living in society. The system was designed to benefit some and exclude others based on our social identities. As I mentioned earlier, we all have some type of social privilege. It might be male privilege, white privilege, heterosexual privilege, physical or psychological privilege, among others. Privilege exists only at the expense of those who don't have it in any given situation. This notion is not academic. It has very real consequences for people's lives, their chance of success, their health and wellbeing.

It is a privilege to feel included and to have a sense of belonging when you come into a room. It is a privilege, for example, to even walk into a room – the physical ability to do so is available to some and not others. And yet, most privilege that provides a sense of inclusion goes unnoticed by those who have it, unless they are asked to reflect on it.

Since Conditioned Self is rooted in Scarcity, it teaches us that we have limited resources and that some people are more deserving of those resources than others. This, however, goes against the notion that we are all drops of water in the ocean – each drop is unique but belongs in the vast body of water called humanity. What might it feel like to know that we all belong? That is not how we are taught to treat people. Most people are raised learning to be kind for the sake of kindness. But what is underneath that superficial kindness? What have we been taught to think about people whose social identities are different than our own?

A lot of healing must occur if we want to get to a place where we all feel welcome and heard. Filmmaker and social justice educator Lee Mun Wah suggests,

> Before we can talk about inclusion, we must first acknowledge the existence and practice of exclusion. And this important conversation requires both whites and people of color engaging with one another and hearing one another's stories and experiences from a place of curiosity instead of a place of fear; understanding instead of denial; self-reflection instead of blaming.

Regardless of our privileges, we have all felt, or have been made to feel, excluded at some point in our lives. According to scholars at the NeuroLeadership Institute, we are evolutionarily primed to fear exclusion. In other words, when we come into a room, our brains are cued to expect to be excluded; someone in the room has to go out of their way to make us feel included for us to feel included.

Or if you look at it from a different perspective: if you are already in the room, and someone comes in, if you do nothing, you are actually reinforcing their feeling of exclusion. The NeuroLeadership Institute's research suggests we have to overcompensate toward inclusive behavior; otherwise people tend to feel excluded. The following mindfulness practice is a good starting point to unpack the feelings associated with these concepts.

MINDFULNESS PRACTICE 16
Connecting with Exclusion and Empowering Ourselves

Get comfortable in a seated position. Breathe. With your eyes closed or gazed down, focus on your inhales and exhales. Let go of any distractions that come into your awareness.

When you are ready, bring into your awareness a time when you have felt excluded. What was the situation? Who was involved? Notice what happens to your body even as you bring up the scenario in your mind. These situations are often triggering for people to experience. Continue to breathe and focus on your breath as you call up the feelings associated with your experience.

Notice where in your body you feel the bulk of the discomfort associated with exclusion. Breathe some loving air into those spaces as you exhale. Inhale, notice, exhale send compassion to those spaces. See if you can soften those triggered places.

Consider that based on social identities, some people feel this exclusionary tension daily, and have this additional challenge no matter which room they enter. No one, not a single drop of water in the ocean of humanity, should have to go through their life feeling this anxiety and discomfort. The messages seep in about our own traditionally marginalized identities as well as those of others. The system continues to reproduce these same tired messages that keep some people included and others excluded.

You have the choice to challenge exclusion when you see it, and to consciously take action to make everyone feel like they belong, to feel included. You have the power to make a difference in this. Inhale that sense of empowerment. Exhale any anxiety that comes up that inhibits your willingness to feel that empowerment or to take action. As you inhale, see if you can straighten up in your seat a little taller; open your chest a bit more if it is available, to breathe in that feeling of empowered intention. Sit with that empowering feeling as long as you like.

When you are ready, take another deep breath, and flutter your eyes open. Stretch your body and take a moment to transition your focus back into the room.

Welcome back.

Feel free to journal now about your experience, or about any ideas or insights that arose for you.

Consider what it might feel like to go into any space and bring your whole self into the room – to truly feel included. We know when people are dealing with stereotype threat, for example, they are not bringing their whole selves into the room. Stereotype threat is when a person's social identity(ies) are cued by their surroundings so they are made to feel excluded. One example is arriving to a meeting and immediately recognizing that you are the only person of your race or the only person of your gender in the room.

When this happens, your social identity can become the focus of your interactions, and you then have to expend extra energy to try to overcome the social stigmas and assumptions that have arisen. The onus then falls on you to exceed others' expectations. This takes precious mental capacity that could otherwise be used to apply your whole mind to innovation or problem-solving. This is one of many arguments in favor of diversity and inclusiveness education or training. Imagine how we could soar if everyone felt like they belonged? This is not the case in most organizations, institutions, and corporations in the U.S.

You know the feeling you get when you are working on a project or trying to explain an inspired, but complicated idea to someone, and suddenly there is a feeling of deep connection with that person, an expanded sense that together, you can move mountains? When this occurs, stereotype threat is lowered; you are both bringing your whole selves in. That is the feeling that mindfulness can create when we have done our work to acknowledge and minimize our biases, welcome and appreciate our differences, and open ourselves to the possibility and opportunities that arise when we mindfully expand our circles. This is hard work; and heart work. Show yourself some compassion as you work through the process.

ACKNOWLEDGING IMPLICIT/UNCONSCIOUS BIAS

We cannot control how others perceive us. But we can challenge the way we have been taught to see others. As troubling as it is to admit, the way we perceive people and treat them is significantly correlated with the stereotypes we hold to be true, even in spite of our best intentions. We may consider ourselves to already be inclusive of others. Unfortunately, we may not be aware that some of the stereotypes we have learned have in fact sunk in, whether we wanted them to or not. Again, the collective cost of our individual biases is not inconsequential. Biases that are acted upon lead to the needless suffering of people with traditionally marginalized identities, even to the point of a shorter lifespan.

Once we are aware of our biases, however, we have a lot of power to mindfully challenge them. In so doing, we minimize those automatic, unconscious, reductive stereotypes and can begin to treat people as the sacred and complex individuals that they are.

In order to challenge our own biases, we must be willing to:
- acknowledge and accept that we all do, in fact, have biases;
- learn what they are;
- mindfully notice when they surface in our thoughts and interactions;
- learn how to challenge them before we act on them; and
- exchange our automatic biases for different, more inclusive, notions.

The most efficient way we have to figure out what our implicit biases are, is to take the free online Implicit Association Tests (IAT) created by Harvard University's Project Implicit. Each quiz takes roughly 5-8 minutes. You simply follow the online instructions and use keys on your keyboard to link words with images as quickly as you can. There are tests on race, gender, sexuality, religious preferences, among others. Your immediate, personalized results are compared with the results of the 5 million other people (as of this writing) who have taken these quizzes. Such a robust subject pool and the fact that these tests have been used by hundreds of peer-reviewed journal articles as a valid way of discovering an individual's implicit bias demonstrates their value in uncovering our biases.

I recommend starting with the test on race, and then proceed through as many of the different tests as you can. If you find you have no bias based on race, you may have bias based on gender or another social identity. We cannot combat our biases unless we know what they are.

Although sometimes difficult to accept the results we are given, from a scientific perspective, the IAT has been shown to give us insight into what we don't know we don't know. It allows us the opportunity to reveal what is going on in our brain and to accept that we have all internalized some potentially disturbing notions.

Many people are resistant to taking these IAT's for fear of what they might learn about themselves. Keep in mind that no matter your race, if you have a strong bias in favor of whites over blacks, it doesn't necessarily mean you are racist, but rather that you have been an excellent student of our culture that was created to perpetuate white supremacist ideologies. We are bombarded with racist messages through the media, school, work, family, and other social institutions. It is in the air we breathe! It means that at least some of those messages have gotten stuck in our brain, through no fault of our own. Since our brains think thoughts, then some of those thoughts are going to be biased. We can mindfully notice them when they arise, without judgment, but with discernment that we can either act on them or not. We have a choice. What will you do once you are aware of your own biases?

It is important to note that the messages we have received from society are so powerful and pervasive that even those with traditionally marginalized social identities (people of color, women, people with disabilities, etc.) show a bias in favor of the dominant group in aggregate IAT data. This is known as internalized oppression, and highlights the importance of uncovering what we don't know about ourselves.

HAND ACTIVITY REVISITED

One way of understanding the effect our biases have on us is to refer back to Juan Diego Estrada's hand activity outlined in Chapter 1. Once again, he suggests putting your hand right in front of your face, if it is available for you to do so. You can't really see anything but your hand, and if you can see through your open fingers, it is from the lens of the biases you have acquired from social conditioning.

Now slowly pull your hand away from your face so that it is about a foot in front of you. All of a sudden, your biases are separate from who you really are. You can see them, but they do not control your situation. Using the Observer in this way means regardless of the results of your IAT, you get to notice when biases arise in you, choose how to respond in any given situation rather than reacting from them based on stereotypes you have learned and no longer want to buy into. With your hand away from your face, you can see many different ways of behaving that are not based on the stereotypes you have learned, such as connecting with the person in front of you from an authentic place.

Professor of Law, John A. Powell, refers to *priming* as one way of challenging the biases we know we have, or have learned we have, from taking the IATs. Priming is thinking of a counter-stereotypic example of someone from the group we know we have a bias against. We can go through this thought process as soon as we learn what our biases are. That way, when we are meeting someone from that group, then we can mindfully and silently call up our counter-stereotypic example in our mind, and research shows that our interactions with that person will be positively affected.

Recent research also informs us that mindfulness practices can counteract Implicit Bias. If implicit bias is also known as unconscious bias, it makes sense that conscious attention (mindfulness) would be an effective way to challenge and disarm our biases. What it takes to challenge our implicit biases is slowing down and acknowledging what is happening in the present moment. If we know what our biases are, we can pause and respond to any situation, rather than react to it. This has positive implications for building authentic, empowered relationships across social differences.

REVISITING KATIE'S FOUR QUESTIONS PLUS ONE

Here, we return to Byron Katie's Four Questions (plus one). Although her work is not based in diversity and inclusiveness, we can take the liberty of applying these questions to stereotypes. We are conditioned to make certain assumptions about people based on their perceived social identities. We can use the following mindfulness practice to challenge our assumptions and biases.

MINDFULNESS PRACTICE 17
Challenging our Assumptions

Get comfortable in a seated position. Breathe. With your eyes closed or gazed down, focus on your inhales and exhales. Let go of any distractions that come into your awareness.

Consider a bias or stereotype you believe is true; perhaps it is one you learned you have subscribed to, based on the results of your IAT. Ask yourself the following questions:

Question One: Is it true? Perhaps based on your limited exposure to this particular group of people, you believe it is, in fact, true.

Question Two: Can you absolutely know that it's true?

Question Three: How do you react? What happens when you believe that thought? What does it feel like in your body? Does the thought give you an expansive, open-hearted feeling, or a closed, contracted feeling? How might this assumption be affecting your interactions and relationships with people from this group?

Question Four: Who would you be without the thought? What might your life/thoughts/actions be without this assumption? What might your interactions be like with people from this social group if you let go of this assumption? What would it feel like in your body to be liberated from this long-held misconception?

When we let go of an idea that no longer serves us, it is often useful to replace it with something useful – perhaps a new idea or positive affirmation. I like to add:

Question Five: What thought or idea could you call to mind to replace your now debunked assumption? What might a different thought be? Consider something positive like, "Every person has beautiful potential."

Make a pact with yourself that the next time you meet someone from this particular social group, you will focus on whatever response you came up with to my fifth question.

When you are ready, take another deep breath, and flutter your eyes open. Stretch your body and take a moment to transition your focus back into the room.

Welcome back.

Feel free to journal now about your experience, or about any ideas or insights that arose for you.

When we challenge a stereotype in our mind before we interact with someone who is a member of a particular social group, we can overcome our biases. Powell suggests that even just by viewing positive images of people from stereotyped groups, and then calling those images into our mind, we can reduce negative biases.

REVISITING "MISTAKES" – MIND THE GAP

What are the implications of implicit or unconscious bias for building relationships across social differences? We are so afraid to make a mistake (to say the "wrong" thing, or to mis-pronoun someone, or to be considered racist) that we avoid interactions with people who have different social identities than we do. Our intention may be honorable; we honestly do not want to offend. The impact, however, is that we are so afraid of making a mistake that we simply do not engage; we segregate ourselves. Our fear of getting out of our comfort zone keeps us separated and isolated. In fact, recall that in terms of housing, the U.S. is more segregated today than it was during the Civil Rights era. Lack of interaction across social differences maintains and perpetuates the myths and stereotypes that we have been taught about other groups, which causes even more mistakes when we do finally decide to engage.

What if we transformed our understanding of what it means to make a "mistake"? What if our mistakes provide us opportunities to learn about people who have different backgrounds and experiences than we do? And just as importantly, what if our mistakes create opportunities to learn more about ourselves?

When we say or do the "wrong" thing and *unintentionally* offend someone based on their social identity, it is known as a microaggression. These comments or behaviors can have dire consequences, especially over a lifetime, particularly for people from traditionally marginalized social groups (people of color, women, LGBTQ - lesbian, gay, bisexual, transgender, queer/questioning individuals, among others). One example of a microaggression is the oft-heard phrase, "that's so gay" to describe something as stupid, silly, ridiculous, etc. Most of the time, it is not meant to offend, but the underlying message is that to be gay is bad or wrong. This phrase has been so pervasive and normalized that those who say it often do not even realize they have said something offensive. The impact can be severe. Yet it can be undone through a lifelong pursuit of unlearning what we have been socialized to believe is acceptable, even appropriate.

Even with the best of intentions, and not meaning to do harm, we will make mistakes along the way. We cannot know everything about all groups. We can only seek to continue to learn and expand our knowledge and understanding. Although the impact of microaggressions can be profound, the fear of microaggressing must not stop us from engaging.

What if we could frame these "mistakes" as a means for building connection instead of causing separation? What if our microaggressions allowed us the opportunity to engage deeply with the person who is impacted most by our action? What might that look like?

Here are some suggestions for handling microaggressions as an opportunity, when, not if, we accidentally "step in it":

Mindfully Focus Inward – Internal Process:

1. Breathe!
2. Acknowledge the "mistake" (either by realizing it or by someone pointing it out to you).
3. Remind yourself that you have dared to engage, and that mistakes are inevitable.
4. Acknowledge whatever you are feeling (embarrassment, defensiveness at being called out, etc.).
5. Allow the shame to surface for a moment, even with the discomfort it brings.
6. Offer yourself some compassion for the shame you might be feeling and the fact that you dared to engage despite the risks.

Mindfully Focus Outward – External Process/Behavior:

7. Verbally offer gratitude to the person who made you aware of the micro-aggression, especially if it is the person who was directly impacted – they were willing to engage with you on this, and respected you enough not to just walk away, hurt, harmed, or offended.
8. Verbally offer a heartfelt apology to the person/people you have offended with no excuses, descriptions, "what I meant was…," or anything else that attempts to explain it away or minimize it – a simple apology is what is needed.
9. Verbally make a promise about future behavior: Let them know you are learning and are committed to doing better in the future.
10. Let it go! Staying stuck in the discomfort inhibits the development of the relationship you are attempting to build.
11. And most importantly, continue to show up in that developing relationship again and again and again in spite of the "mistake."

When someone makes me aware of a microaggression I have committed, such as mis-gendering a transgender person, for example, my first response, once I have internally and mindfully acknowledged and processed the discomfort and shame I am feeling, is: "Thank you for trusting our relationship enough to stay in it and let me know what I didn't know." I do not want to put the onus on the person who I have offended to teach me what I have done wrong. Yet when we have committed to building relationships across social differences, we end up with many people around us whom we trust, who trust us, and whom we have invited to gently challenge us. They can guide us – whether they are the direct recipients of our microaggressions or allies of the recipients.

One way to easily remember your outward response/behavior once you have completed the internal process is based on the often-heard caution that is broadcast in the Tube stations (subway) of London. They say "Mind the GAP" which reminds travelers to step cautiously between the station plank and the traincar. I use it here because it helps us to first and foremost, proceed *mindfully* across the gap we have just created between ourselves and the person against whom we have just impacted from our microaggression. Secondly, consider the word GAP as an acronym:

- Gratitude
- Apology
- Promise

This can come in handy the next time you make a so-called "mistake" based on a social identity. It is an important part of the process of building authentic relationships across social differences, and can deepen and strengthen those relationships.

As Maya Angelou said, "When we know better, we do better." That is a commitment worth making. Imagine if we were not stifled by our fear of making mistakes. Imagine if we were committed to learning and growing trusting relationships across social differences. Consider what might open up in our lives by doing so.

SO-CALLED "MICROAGGRESSIONS:" GOING DEEPER

In his book, *Microaggressions in Everyday Life*, Dr. Derald Wing Sue describes microaggressions as subtle comments and/or behaviors that insult, invalidate, or exclude others in spite of good intentions. They tend to cue stereotypes based on a person's social identity, and create an "us" vs. "them" dynamic where the perpetrator takes insider-status, and the person against whom the microaggression is aimed is thrust into outsider-status. The concept of Colorblindness, as discussed in Chapter 3, "Mindfulness in Context and Spiritual Bypassing," is an example of a microaggression, such as when a white person says to a person of color, "I don't see color; we're all human."

In my mind, the difference between microaggressions and outright racism, sexism, heterosexism, etc., is the intention of the perpetrator. If the perpetrator means to do harm, their actions would not be considered "micro." This does not mean the impact of both micro and macro aggressions aren't comparably harmful. In fact, there is nothing subtle or micro about so-called microaggressions. In other words, it is important to ask: subtle to whom? These acts may seem subtle to the perpetrator who has no explicit intention of causing harm; however, for the recipient, subtlety is not an accurate or appropriate descriptor.

Microaggressions are often brushed off by the perpetrator as "just a joke" or "I didn't mean it that way; don't be so sensitive!" The impact of these actions is not inconsequential; they can affect the recipient's sense of belonging, trust, performance, chance of success, and can create a hostile environment. Dr. Sue found that microaggressions can also manifest in the recipient's body in the form of physiological stress, anxiety, diminished cognitive functioning, and over the course of a lifetime, can cause higher mortality rates for members of traditionally marginalized groups.

Despite the deleterious effects of microaggressions, they often go unchallenged. Unfortunately, not responding only serves to maintain and perpetuate a hostile environment. We can use mindfulness practices to challenge microaggressions effectively. First, it is important, whenever possible, to come from a place of assuming positive intent. In many instances, this can be difficult to do; even witnessing microaggressions, whether or not they are directed at us, can be jarring and cause a reaction within us. Assuming positive intent will make it more likely that you will successfully respond. The following mindfulness practice provides a technique for responding to a microaggression when you are a bystander, or as I like to say, an Upstander.

MINDFULNESS PRACTICE 18
Successfully Interrupting Microaggressions:
Pause-Notice-Breathe-Respond

Get comfortable in a seated position. Breathe. With your eyes closed or gazed down, focus on your inhales and exhales. Let go of any distractions that come into your awareness.

When you feel fully present in this moment, consider a situation in which you have witnessed someone making an extremely offensive comment. Keep clear in your mind what it was they said and how you felt when they said it.

Pause. Notice *what is happening inside your body. Acknowledge any tension you are feeling. Are you feeling agitated?* ***Breathe:*** *Inhale deeply, and as you exhale, see if you can release even the smallest amount of tension. Be* aware that you are likely feeling triggered by the situation, and that this is a normal human experience. If you need a few more deep breaths, take them. Offer yourself some compassion for experiencing such a challenging situation. Use the Observer if you need to, and know that as frustrating or harmful as this microaggression is, you are more than your reaction. And you have the power to mindfully take action.

Gently and purposefully responding rather than aggressively reacting is the key to a successful interaction, and can increase the chances that the person will engage with you rather than become defensive. Consider what would be the most effective way to **Respond** to the person who just made the hurtful comment. What can you say to call the person in rather than calling them out? If they begin to lean in, it is likely that they want to learn more about why you found their comment hurtful. That is one way to know you are successful. Keep in mind, even if you engage in the most compassionate way you can, the other person may not be open to your intervention. Even if they respond brusquely, they may still be thinking about your comment later. Rarely does someone change their mind the moment they hear a new perspective.

When you are ready, take another deep breath, and flutter your eyes open. Stretch your body and take a moment to transition your focus back into the room.

Welcome back.

Feel free to journal now about your experience, or about any ideas or insights that arose for you.

The next time you witness a microaggression (*when*, not *if*), consider using this mindfulness practice. If the microaggression was not directed at you, but rather to someone nearby, be sure to pause before responding to provide space for the intended recipient to respond themselves. A good culturally inclusive practice is to make sure you are not disempowering someone to respond for themselves. A participant in one workshop suggested asking the person to whom the microaggression was aimed, "Do you want to take this, or should I?" I like this idea.

As an inclusive leadership practice, it is important to always respond gently but publicly to microaggressions. Not responding affirms that offensive comments or behaviors are allowed and acceptable. This can contribute to a hostile environment for people from traditionally marginalized groups, and their advocates.

Simply pausing before responding in any situation is a mindfulness practice you can make use of throughout your day. It is a positive health/wellness technique, as well as an important strategy for building relationships across social differences.

CHAPTER 10

Mindfulness for Cultural Inclusion – Connecting across Differences

"It is not our differences that divide us. It is our inability to recognize, accept, and celebrate those differences." ~Audre Lorde

My dear friend, Norma, and I were having lunch together one day. We were talking about how important but challenging it is to build relationships across social differences. We are both social justice educators; she is African American and I am white. We both agreed that when people hear about diversity and inclusion training, or are required to attend by their organization or corporation, they are reluctant at best, resistant at worst. We are constantly fighting an uphill battle just to get in the room because, as I know from my national research, we already think we are prepared to build cultural inclusion – we don't believe we need any training.

Norma suggested we come at it from a different angle. She said most people have no idea what they are missing from living a mono-cultural life. She started talking about the joy that building relationships across social differences has brought her. How her life has expanded beyond measure because of some of those relationships. They are not without their challenges, of course, but the bottom line is, this is something we never talk about – the joy that doing diversity and inclusion work brings! She suggested we need to see more examples of cross-cultural relationships, and the beauty, love, and joy that can be shared within those relationships.

I got the same message from Peggy McIntosh, author of the ground-breaking work, "Unpacking the Invisible Knapsack" (a must read, if you are not familiar). Peggy told me that before she was aware of the system of inequalities that impact all of our lives, and before she was aware of her own social privilege, she had no idea what she was missing. She likened her life experience to a pie. She said she didn't know she was only getting a sliver of all that is possible in the human experience. As she started to travel more, and have more multicultural experiences, and meet more people who didn't share her social identities, she could see more and more of the pie. She felt she began to live life much more fully.

Mindfulness practices are a way of doing our own work as a precursor to building healthy, culturally inclusive relationships. These practices allow us to make obvious what's not, and acknowledge and attend to our own biases and behaviors. We can implement mindfulness practices to build and develop cross-cultural relationships, too. Although society has done a great job of keeping us segregated and it is nothing short of trying to climb up Niagra Falls to build these strong relationships across difference, it is not impossible. In order to expand our experience in the world and live large, we must begin within.

RELATIONSHIP INVENTORY

To reflect on how this system of segregation has impacted you, you can start by taking a quick inventory of your closest friends. Conditioned Self has taught us to make friends with people whose lives and social identities are similar to our own. We are taught that it is most prudent to associate with people who, even on the surface, seem like they would best be able to relate to our own lives. However, following this social conditioning leads us to live very isolated and segregated lives. We are missing out on the richness that humanity has to offer.

I invite you to reflect on your most intimate relationships. With whom do you share your life? With whom do you feel you can always be yourself? Who are the people that have earned the right to hear your story? Who are those you might call when you are feeling vulnerable or shameful that you know will be compassionate to you? What are their social identities (their races, genders, sexualities, physical abilities, mental abilities, ages, etc.)? Are they similar or different than yours? What factors have encouraged these relationships? Are there any relationships that you worked harder than others to keep? If so, why?

Reflecting on these kinds of questions allows us to start from within to see the impact of our socialization and to see how social conditioning may have nudged us in a certain direction that maintains segregation in our society. If you consider your life to be multicultural, know that in the U.S., you have had and/or have chosen an extraordinary life – it is not the norm.

MINDFUL RELATIONSHIPS ACROSS DIFFERENCES

We are constantly bombarded with biases and stereotypes from all the messages we consume in a given day, and those stereotypes become so ingrained in us that when we meet someone whose social identities are different than our own, we think we already know so much about them. This is problematic, especially when trying to build deep connections across differences. Clearing your head with a quick mindfulness practice of remembering Beginner's Mind is sometimes all it takes to start a new relationship with someone without the baggage of preconceived notions. If you recall from the Introduction, Beginner's Mind is the practice of coming into any situation with an "I don't know and I'm open to learn" mentality, with humility.

Rather than spending precious cognitive energy making judgments or challenging our judgments about the person with whom we are speaking, using Beginner's Mind, those stereotypes recede into the background as we wholeheartedly engage, paying close attention to what the person before us is saying. With an "empty," curious mind (a "Beginner's Mind"), we may be less likely to stereotype, judge, or make assumptions about the person we are in conversation with. Moreover, we may be less likely to make assumptions about the person/people/subject they are speaking about. We are connecting in a more genuine way that will serve to build trust and stronger, healthier relationships.

When we are able to connect to our Inspired Self through mindfulness practices, we gain the opportunity to show up and engage in the world from an authentic place, without pretense or agenda. It allows us to project the best part of ourselves. When we do so, we connect deeply with others.

When I think about the self-reflection and the revolutionary act of building relationships across differences, I am always reminded of Pat Parker's words of wisdom from her poem, "For the White Person Who Wants to Know How to Be My Friend." Parker writes, "The first thing you do is to forget that i'm Black; Second, you must never forget that i'm Black." I would argue that this lesson could be applied to any social identity. In other words, Parker is suggesting: be aware of my social identities, have some knowledge about them, and then treat me as a human being rather than as the sum total of my differences. This goes beyond political correctness. It is a commitment to genuinely creating authentic, respectful relationships across difference.

I offer a few suggestions for building relationships across social identity differences, and you can find many more in my book, *The Culturally Inclusive Educator.*

BRINGING IT ALL TOGETHER

The following mindfulness practice offers the opportunity to connect concepts from the last few chapters and to experience the embodiment of cultural exclusion and inclusion.

MINDFULNESS PRACTICE 19
Connecting the Spiritual with the Physical

Get comfortable in a seated position. Breathe. With your eyes closed or gazed down, focus on your inhales and exhales. Allow whatever thoughts come into your mind to come and go without dwelling on them. If any thought seems to get stuck or grab your attention, remind yourself that it is just a thought and need not be followed. If it persists, simply offer it gratitude for coming into your awareness and let it go.

Now, turn your focus on your Inner Light. Allow it to expand. From that space, picture your body around the light, your feet on the ground, walking on the earth. You are on the terrain – looking out through the eyes of the human body your Inner Light is inhabiting. What do you see? Can you look up and see the expanse of the sky? Do you see trees blowing in the peaceful breeze? Do you see the desert sand scorched red by the hot sun? Do you see the ocean before you? This is the earth we inhabit.

You begin to see the natural diversity that exists here on this planet. You see the different colors, the different forms of life. From this vantage point, you can see that everything is alive. You can appreciate all the beauty and can experience the overwhelming emotions brought on by your connection to all that you are beholding. Your Inner Light expands to embrace and appreciate it all.

And then there, in the distance, you see another human form slowly walking towards you. You are in such a high level of energy or vibration, that you are excited to share your joy and love with the person who is entering your awareness.

As the person slowly approaches, their features start to become clearer. You notice that their appearance is very different from the way you perceive yourself to appear. Their gender is different than yours; their skin color is different; they have a different hair form; and their clothes insinuate a very different socio-economic status than yours.

Before you know it, your mind is filled with all that you have been conditioned to believe about someone who looks like this person. You want to share your experience of all the beauty in the world, but you are stifled by fear and mistrust. Your mind starts to imagine the worst of this person: that they might be out to get you or that they mean you harm. And based on their conditioning about someone who looks like you, they may be afraid, too, or worse, actually mean to do you harm.

Pause. Check in with your body. Where in your body do you feel this fear of "the Other"? Just notice it. What is the sense of it? Do you feel open or constricted? How likely is it that with this fear in your body, you will be able to engage openly with this person?

This fear of "the Other" is what sparked the systems of inequality that have benefited some at the expense of others. It is at the root of the Conditioned Self and is motivated by power, greed, and the desire to control.

Once you can recognize this learned fear of people whose social identities are different from yours, you can call it what it is: Conditioned Self. It is simply a conglomeration of thoughts that keep us separated from each other. Just like before, you can offer those thoughts gratitude for showing up – even if you can see now that they no longer serve you – offer gratitude for giving you the opportunity to acknowledge they have been stuck inside you and now, you can let them go. After all, this person simply represents a reflection of you; another drop of water in the ocean of humanity.

What thought might you replace that conditioned assumption you had about that person in order to be able to interact authentically with them? What might be a positive affirmation that will minimize the impact of Conditioned Self and allow you to engage openly, deeply, authentically? Whatever affirmation you come up with, repeat it several times. Breathe it in.

When you are ready, take another deep breath, and flutter your eyes open. Stretch your body and take a moment to transition your focus back into the room.

Welcome back.

Feel free to journal now about your experience, or about any ideas or insights that arose for you.

If we set an intention to challenge Conditioned Self to break free from the stereotypes we have about each other and dare to engage, how different would our lives be? How can we begin to create or build an already culturally inclusive life with deep, authentic relationships across differences? And what if those differences are based on different worldviews?

CULTURE CLASH: MINDFULLY ENGAGING
ACROSS POLITICAL DIFFERENCES

I was speaking to a large group of people recently about racial justice and the importance of learning about what we don't know we don't know. Many people in the room were leaning in, wanting more. They knew what we all know: that in the current state of affairs, we will need better strategies of engaging people whose worldviews or perspectives are different from our own.

After the talk, I was approached by a white man who told me something I hear often in my line of work: racism is over; we are living in a post-racial society now. I braced myself for the conversation to come, and I remembered all of my mindfulness tools. I took a deep breath, looked him right in the eye, and nodded. My first instinct was to go into full-blown lecture mode with all the proof of how wrong he is. But I caught myself, knowing from experience how ineffective that strategy would be.

I chose instead to pause and breathe. I watched as his stare hardened, and he looked poised for a fight. I took another deep breath, looked him right in the eye to connect, to find his humanity, and I calmly said, "You know, I'm not trying to make me right and you wrong." He stopped himself in mid-harangue and his jaw dropped in disbelief. Softening, he eased his stance. And we continued our conversation. He leaned in, asked me some questions, asked me for further resources to learn more. It was a successful encounter. I could tell he felt heard, and was open to learning new information.

Afterwards, I thought that next time, I would mention social justice educator, activist, and speaker Jane Elliott's brilliant counter to the idea that racism is over. She often asks her packed audiences, "How many of you white folks would trade places with a black person today?" And she waits. And the only sound is that of the people of color in the room turning in their chairs to see if anyone will raise their hand. And she waits. And not a single white person raises their hand. And she says, "You know what you just admitted? That this is happening, and you don't want it for you. So why are you so willing for it to be the case for someone else?"

Although it might be disturbing for folks of color to hear and witness, it cuts through to how deep and insidious white privilege is. And how unwilling some white folks are to talk about it or even consider that it exists. And so, we must be prepared to engage in these conversations effectively.

The following are some mindful strategies for the next time you find yourself in a dialogue across differences, especially if you are coming to the conversation from a place of power/a privileged identity (i.e., a male person challenging someone on sexist behavior; a white person challenging someone on racist behavior; a person without disabilities challenging someone on able-ist behavior, a heterosexual person challenging someone on heterosexist or homophobic behavior, etc.):

1. Stay calm and breathe.
2. Mindfully come to the conversation with respect and compassion.
3. Find a way to authentically connect with the person (eye contact, for example, although that would not be appropriate in all situations or cultures).
4. Let go of being "right" or you will end up in a tug of war that is unwinnable.
5. Meet them where they're at as opposed to asserting your point of view.
6. Genuinely seek to understand their point of view; gently inquire about how they came to their conclusions; you might be surprised what you learn.
7. Bring your passion about social justice, without being overbearing;
8. Use examples of how these issues affect you personally; why do you care?
9. Use the Platinum Rule: treat others as they want to be treated.
10. Keep in mind: you can't "flip every pancake," or in other words, you can't convince every person that you are right – you will burn out trying; and it's ok that you can't; it is better to move on and use your energy where it will be better received.

And how do you know when you're successful?

1. If the conversation doesn't end with this one "confrontation."
2. If the other person leans in and shows curiosity.
3. If you let go of trying to be "right" and engage with them.
4. If the other person stops trying to be "right" and engages with you.
5. If the other person asks for resources to learn more.
   The goal is not to establish a kumbaya relationship. That is neither

possible nor desired. You don't need to become best friends with the other person. Rather, it's a matter of shared humanity. Showing up with deep respect and dignity no matter the other person's ideology. Call them in rather than calling them out.

Know that these conversations can be challenging. And rest assured, they will continue to happen more and more. Be ready. The more prepared you are, the more successful you will be connecting, respecting, and empathizing mindfully across different perspectives.

Lastly, we can mindfully connect across social or political differences from a place of love. Love is always in divine alignment and operates with divine intention. When our perspectives or worldviews are being challenged, remember to pause and then respond from a place of love – you have a choice to either *react* based on social conditioning or to *respond* in alignment with your highest self; living from the inside out means you get to behave as you want to show up regardless of the situation you are facing.

MINDFULLY OPENING YOUR HEART
FOR COMPASSIONATE CONNECTIONS

A few months ago, I was on an airport shuttle from long-term parking to the terminal. I was headed to a university on the east coast to present two days of keynotes and workshops. All of a sudden, the woman in the seat in front of me began sneezing uncontrollably. It went on and on and on. My first thought was self-preservation. I couldn't afford to catch a cold so I started to cover my mouth so I wouldn't breathe in what I could only imagine was her toxic germs. I began to get more and more frustrated at the woman. How dare she expose me to these germs? (Not my proudest moment, I admit!). And then, suddenly, I remembered my mindfulness practice. I took a deep breath in and began to acknowledge and appreciate the suffering she was experiencing. My heart literally opened to her, and I began to silently wish her health and wellbeing.

Literally, the moment I began this practice, her sneezing stopped. I continued my practice, incredulously, as she turned to her fellow passengers and said, "Wow, I must be allergic to something on this bus; I hope I didn't bother anyone with my sneezing." True story! She had not been sick at all but was having an acute allergic reaction to something on the bus. Although I had concern for her discomfort, I had absolutely nothing to worry about in regards to my own health.

As difficult as it is to share this story – I am truly ashamed of the thoughts that went through my head – it was such a revelation to me once I was able to pause and reflect on where my thoughts had immediately gone. I went straight to fear and wanted to distance myself from this woman. Self-preservation may be a strong evolutionary tendency in humans, but my outright frustration at this poor woman was neither humane nor compassionate. As soon as I opened my heart to her, to the moment, her suffering was alleviated. Could you call this coincidental? Sure. Either way, I hope the lesson I learned is not lost. It was a powerful turning point in my mindfulness practice.

What I offered this woman was the mindfulness meditation called Metta, or Lovingkindness. It is a well-known Buddhist practice that not only boosts the energy of the person to whom you offer the mantra, but it has also been shown to boost your own energy. This practice can be useful for healing negative feelings that you might have towards any person in your life. I will offer four stages of the practice: first, focusing on a loved one; second, focusing on those people around you to whom you are ambivalent or don't have strong feelings about one way or the other; third, focusing on a person toward whom you retain negative feelings; and fourth, focusing on yourself and all living beings.

MINDFULNESS PRACTICE 20
Metta/Lovingkindness

Get comfortable in a seated position. Breathe. With your eyes closed or gazed down, focus on your inhales and exhales. Let go of any distractions that come into your awareness.

When you are ready, focus on someone you love; someone who brightens your day simply by entering the room you are in. Focus on that person. Notice what happens in your body when you consider this person. Do you feel your heart opening? Do you get an expansive feeling in your chest or your body? Do you automatically smile?

Now, slowly, silently offer this person Metta or Lovingkindness:
May you be well.
May you be happy.
May you be free from suffering.
May you live with ease.
Notice what happens in your own body as you offer this Metta. This

*meditation can often bring a warm sense of peace. Sit with that feeling as long
as you like.*

*When you are ready, call to mind someone in your life who you don't know
well; perhaps you would like to get to know them better, but for now, they
are on the sidelines of your life or bystanders you pass on the street. Perhaps
even think of yourself walking down a street and you notice the people around
you. You can cultivate connection simply by opening your own heart in their
direction.*

Now, slowly, silently offer those around you Metta or Lovingkindness:
May you be well.
May you be happy.
May you be free from suffering.
May you live with ease.

*Notice any effects this practice has on you, your body, or even your own
sense of well-being.*

*Now, when you are ready, call to mind someone with whom you have had
some challenges in the past. It could be from years ago or someone with whom
you had a recent disagreement that brought about negative feelings or residual
negativity toward this person. If this is your first time with this practice, I
recommend starting with someone who has not done severe harm, but rather
toward whom you feel a mild discontent or unrest.*

*Notice what happens in your body as you focus on this person. Does your
posture change at all? Does your heart feel a little more contracted? Perhaps
that feeling comes out of self-preservation? Remember, it is perfectly fine to
protect yourself – we don't have to sacrifice our own wellbeing for another's
– we are simply focusing on the impact the negativity has on our own bodies.
That is the energy that no longer serves us that we can begin to release with this
practice.*

*Without getting caught up in the situation that caused your negative
feelings about this person, see if instead, when you are ready, you can offer this
person Metta. Sometimes this takes a bit of a paradigm shift. Know that you
are in no way condoning their behavior, but rather attempting to alleviate your
own suffering from carrying the weight of the impact they have thrust upon
you. Know that if they hurt you or someone else, they were hurt. This is one
step toward alleviating suffering in you, and in the world.*

Slowly, silently offer this person Metta or Lovingkindness:
May you be well.

May you be happy.

May you be free from suffering.

May you live with ease.

Notice any release at all in your body. Is there even the slightest bit of expansion compared with the contraction you felt before? If so, you are on your way to healing – not for them, but for you.

Finally, recognize that you are a human being. You are one of the billions of living beings that are currently alive and breathing on this planet. This includes other humans, animals, plants, etc.

Slowly, silently offer yourself and all living beings Metta or Lovingkindness:

May I and all living beings be well.

May I and all living beings be happy.

May I and all living beings be free from suffering.

May I and all living beings live with ease.

When you are ready, take another deep breath, and flutter your eyes open. Stretch your body and take a moment to transition your focus back into the room.

Welcome back.

Feel free to journal now about your experience, or about any ideas or insights that arose for you.

Metta meditation can be extremely beneficial for our own health and wellbeing. It allows us to release stale, negative emotions and energy that have been stored in our bodies. Metta is a powerful tool to use in many situations. I often use it when I am driving and someone cuts me off. As soon as I can breathe through the adrenaline rush that instantly surges through me, I remember my practice and offer the person Metta. It is like a salve that makes me feel more physically and emotionally steady, much more loving and open-hearted toward the person, and more at peace in general. In fact, when I am feeling down, as soon as I start offering Metta to those around me, I feel better.

Metta is a phenomenal resource, and a mindfulness practice that is useful on an interpersonal level; we now turn to the ways mindfulness can be utilized to raise awareness and challenge inequities in our social institutions at the systemic level.

CHAPTER 11

Mindfulness for Social Justice

"Let us be the ancestors our descendants will thank." ~Winona LaDuke

In co-facilitating workshops with my friend/colleague, Stephany, we often find that participants are unclear on the differences between diversity, cultural inclusion, and social justice. We ask participants to think about **diversity** as the differences between us based on race, gender, social class, sexuality, age, among others. **Cultural inclusion** means welcoming all of those social identities so that every person feels like they belong. **Social justice** refers to the act of examining and challenging the social systems that privilege some at the expense of others.

Stephany uses the analogy of the holiday table. When she gets together with her family, she finds that there is a *diverse* set of guests: meat-lovers, vegetarians, vegans, etc. *Cultural inclusion* acknowledges the needs of each guest and welcomes all, letting each know that they will have something delicious to eat that they will enjoy when they arrive. *Social justice* asks: who has access to holiday dinners and who does not? Which social systems make it more likely that the meat-lovers will be provided for more easily and less expensively than the vegetarians or vegans? Who decides? Who is most impacted by the production, distribution, and health outcomes of meat? What can we do to make a difference in this area? This chapter focuses on these latter questions: using mindfulness practices for challenging the systems in place that include some and exclude others.

One of those systems is our justice system in the U.S. "I can't breathe" were Eric Garner's last words at the hands of NYPD police officer Daniel

Pantaleo, and they became the rallying cry for the Black Lives Matter movement in 2014. He wasn't the first nor the last Black man to be killed at the hands of police, but his last words provide a metaphor for the legacy of the system of inequality that was put in place centuries ago and remains intact today. This system is in the air we *all* breathe. It is the remnants of the contaminants of the air created by white people for white people. It is recycled in all of our institutions: our schools, media, families, legislature, healthcare, legal systems, religious centers, among others. Challenging and working to dismantle the system of privilege and domination that informs all of our lives is at the root of social justice work.

In Chapter 7, "Mindfully Discovering What Stops Us," I mentioned that the first step in yoga is to acknowledge how your body feels today so you can meet it where it's at as a launching point. The first step in social justice is to acknowledge the impact that institutionalized privilege and discrimination has had on our lives, and the social conditioning that has kept it going. This is the launching point for social justice work.

UNPLUGGING FROM THE MATRIX

One way of understanding these concepts is through the first installment of the incredibly profound and popular film series, *The Matrix Trilogy* (Wachowski, 1999), when Laurence Fishburne's character, Morpheus, explains to Neo, played by Keanu Reeves, what The Matrix is. He says,

> "The Matrix is everywhere, it's all around us, here even in this room. You can see it out your window or on your television. You feel it when you go to work, or go to church or pay your taxes. It is the world that has been pulled over your eyes to blind you from the truth... Like everyone else, you were born into bondage, kept inside a prison that you cannot smell, taste, or touch. A prison for your mind. (pp. 28-29)

Morpheus goes on to explain:

> "The Matrix is a system, Neo, and that system is our enemy. But when you are inside and you look around, what do you see; businessmen, lawyers, teachers, carpenters... You have to understand that most of these people are not ready to be unplugged [from The Matrix] and many of them are so inured, so hopelessly dependent on the system that they will fight to protect it... they are the gatekeepers, they're guarding

all the doors, holding all the keys, which means that sooner or later
someone is going to have to fight them. (pp. 53-54, Retrieved from
http://www.dailyscript.com/scripts/the_matrix.pdf 3/10/18)

If we think of The Matrix as social conditioning, then to "unplug" from
The Matrix means to first notice we are products of our social conditioning,
and then to mindfully decide if we want to continue to collude with it, or
challenge it. Mindfulness practices can serve as tools for acknowledging all
forms of privilege/unearned advantage and oppression/disadvantage when
we witness them, in ourselves, in others, and/or in institutions or organizations. To speak up and speak out against the system of inequalities is doing
the work of social justice.

REVISITING SINGER'S DARK BOX:
MINDFULLY DISMANTLING SYSTEMIC PRIVILEGE

We begin within. Let us unpack this system of privilege and how it affects
all of us by revisiting Singer's Dark Box from Chapter 4, "Mindfulness to
Discover the Wisdom Our Bodies Hold." If you recall, the analogy likened
the challenges we have personally faced to living in a dark box, and the only
way out is to first recognize we are actually stuck in a dark box, and to face
and process the discomfort that comes with touching the edges of the box.
This is where the lightness pours in.

What if we were to take this analogy and apply it to the system of
inequality that we live in? What if the dark box in this case represented the
system of white supremacist ideology and elitism we have been conditioned
in? It is the air we all breathe and it is a box we are trapped in. The box is
not made up of only white supremacist ideology, it also includes ideologies
of heterosexism, patriarchy, ableism, classism, among others. It is a box of
social privilege. And keep in mind, we all have some sort of privilege. We
have been conditioned to ignore the privilege that we have, just as we have
been conditioned to ignore the air we breathe. This box of privilege is toxic
because it is only maintained at the expense of anyone whose identity does
not fit in the box (people in poverty, people of color, people who identify as
LGBTQ, older folks, among others).

Every now and then, someone provides us a crack in the box by showing
us what we're missing by being stuck in the box of privilege. The box has
kept us from knowing there was anything outside the box that was worthy of

our time or attention.

When a crack in the box is formed, we are drawn to the light, but once again, the light seems to illuminate the white supremacist (and other privileged) ideals that we have been taught to obey, and that have seeped into our pores. The light highlights all the stories we have been told about the supposed inherent benefits that come with white skin, maleness, heterosexuality, or other forms of privilege. The light shows the benefits of unearned trust and goodness that are birthrights of dominant culture in this society – and the disadvantages of being born with any identity that doesn't match that ideal. We have been taught this; we are conditioned to believe these myths. It allows those in power to stay in power. This is the reason this system was created. And it works perfectly.

And yet, as we remain in the dark box, just as Morpheus explains, we are forced to perpetuate this system. Not only at other people's expense, but also at our own. We are missing out. We are keeping ourselves in a box that no longer serves us, and we can feel it. It takes a toll on our own health and wellbeing when we sense something is very wrong. Privilege allows us to ignore the box, but as Morpheus describes the *truth* in The Matrix, he refers to it as "a splinter in your mind." This analogy fits perfectly. Those who were raised to stay inside the box and not stray were given the impression that the box exists to keep them safe from outsiders. What if instead, the box is imprisoning us?

As we get closer to the edge of the box, we are forced to face how these dangerous myths have seeped into our pores. And it is incredibly uncomfortable. Feelings of fear and shame and trepidation come up. If we are truly committed to our own health and wellbeing, then we will choose to feel the discomfort anyway. Because that is the only way we can both traverse the walls of the box, and mindfully dismantle them. As we allow ourselves to feel the emotions that have been trapped inside us, to acknowledge our privileged identities and how they have kept us isolated and afraid of difference, the walls melt away and we are one step closer to a just world.

I am not suggesting that if we choose to overcome the privilege within us that privilege will no longer exist. The system is structural, and as much as we might desire the fairness that comes with dismantling an unequal system, we cannot opt out of the system. No matter how fairly we perceive ourselves or treat others, what impacts our lives is how others perceive and treat us. If they perceive that we have privilege, they will treat us as such. Nevertheless, this fact does not absolve us from doing the work necessary to acknowledge and extract the ways in which privilege (which we all have) has manifested within us.

AGAIN, WITH THE HAND

Remember, we have been taught not to see our own privilege. It is so normalized, it is difficult to perceive. We can once again implement a revised version of Estrada's hand activity to recognize our privilege. What if your hand represents the privilege/unearned benefits you have been awarded based on a social identity? If it is available to you, put your hand in front of your face. Allow it to represents one of your privileged identities. As you use your Observer, you can pull the hand away from your face and notice that you do, in fact, operate through a privileged lens. Pulling your hand away does not remove the privilege within you – that is not the way the system works. It does, however, offer you the space to see how your privilege operates, and increases your capacity to challenge it when you see it. Even after the fact, if not in the moment.

Recently, I attended the annual White Privilege Conference. It's a social justice conference founded and directed by Dr. Eddie Moore, Jr., that I have helped to organize for almost 15 years. I was mesmerized by the powerful keynote speaker, Dr. Bettina Love. She brought up some ideas that I applied to my own work as she was speaking. I wondered how mindfulness practices might alleviate suffering in communities that do not yet have access to them and how these practices might be of service. I was so caught up in this thought that before Dr. Love even left the stage, I had turned to my friend, Norma, who was sitting nearby, and began to bombard her with my own reflections on the presentation. I mindlessly barraged her with my questions and concerns before she even had a chance to absorb or digest the presentation herself. My white privilege got the better of me as my reflections became more important and pressing than my black friend's. This is one way in which unearned entitlement operates.

I wish I could say I noticed or caught my behavior while it was happening. I did not. It was a full twenty-four hours later during a meditation that it dawned on me that my behavior was a symptom of a system of white supremacist ideology playing out. Feeling shame for just a moment, I was able to process the emotions, offer myself some compassion for a difficult situation, and immediately sent a message to Norma with an apology, no excuses, and a promise to continue to work on unpacking my white privilege.

She readily accepted my apology, and we moved on, secure in our ongoing friendship. Unpacking and dismantling privilege is a lifelong journey; yet one that is possible. It is critically important that we both recognize when it happens (or soon thereafter) and acknowledge it out loud. This brings hope that a better future is possible.

Let's consider how we can begin to challenge, and work toward dismantling the dark box of systemic privilege. We start with awareness of how it affects us all on a daily basis.

MINDFULNESS PRACTICE 21
Acknowledging the Impact of an Unfair System

Get comfortable in a seated position. Breathe. With your eyes closed or gazed down, focus on your inhales and exhales. Let go of any distractions that come into your awareness.

Begin by finding your anchor. Something or someone in your life that makes you feel happy, light, grounded; anything that reminds you that you are whole. Stay with the feelings that come up as long as you like. Continue to breathe in those feelings. They give you strength.

When you are ready, consider for a moment any of the social identities you have that carry privileged-status in society (being male, white, heterosexual, mentally or physically able, among others). You may not feel the privilege associated with these identities because we have been systematically taught not to. Remember, that ignoring our privilege insures that the system as it was created will be maintained.

Try to tap into where in your body you feel the weight of privilege. This might take some time, and some practice. Your Conditioned Self might even be screaming that you don't have any privilege, or that it is not your fault, or why should you feel bad for having any privilege? The goal is not to feel badly or guilty for being given any of your unearned advantages, for you did not create the system that benefits some at the expense of others. It is important to connect, and connect deeply with the emotions that we are taught to stifle around these issues, so that healing can occur.

Whether or not you are new to this idea that we all have some form of social privilege, consider the impact it has on your life. What does it mean you are able to do on a daily basis that others might not? What emotions arise from simply knowing this is so? Again, the goal is not guilt, but rather to feel the heaviness that is caused by an unfair system.

What emotions emerge from focusing on the unfair system in which we live? Frustration, perhaps? Anger? Sadness? Guilt? Other emotions? Where do you feel those emotions in your body? In your chest? In your gut? Somewhere else?

As you breathe, offer some compassion to those spaces in your body that feel or hold that heaviness. You did not cause this system to be as it is. Feel whatever comes up for you. And see if you can stay open to the idea that you can in fact be an agent of change and alleviate your own and others' suffering. The unfair systems are made up of people. Sit with the question of: How can I make a difference? Sit with this question as long as you like. And know that you have the power to make a difference.

When you are ready, take another deep breath, and flutter your eyes open. Stretch your body and take a moment to transition your focus back into the room.

Welcome back.

Feel free to journal now about your experience, or about any ideas or insights that arose for you.

Stay with the question of: How can I make a difference? as you continue through this chapter. Let the question marinate in you. Strategies and suggestions will be offered along the way that might spark your own innovative approach. One thing we can all do is to pay close attention whenever we see injustice and make the invisible, visible. As we have all heard, "If you see something, say something!" Don't let injustice or discrimination, even if it seems subtle to you, go unchallenged.

MINDFULLY CHALLENGING INEQUITIES IN OUR INSTITUTIONS

Leading edge research indicates that to challenge implicit bias effectively, we must broaden our scope beyond just personal change. The NeuroLeadership Institute recommends we focus both on personal and organizational/institutional change. We must acquire an awareness of how bias manifests in our own brains and how it operates in organizations in ways that make it more likely that we will engage in exclusionary behavior. This has great impact for making important decisions like hiring, promotion, among others.

Mindful practices can help leaders to slow down and consider organizational practices that might help to minimize bias such as: creating rubrics for hiring to ensure every candidate is asked the same questions, making sure all candidates are interviewed the same way (all by telephone, and/or all by teleconference, and/or all in person), and making sure to have a hiring committee rather than having the decisions made by one person. There are many other strategies that can assist in mitigating implicit bias and challenge the systems that have consistently made some feel included and others excluded. Beyond creating change within an organization, consider the ways inequities operate in the many institutions we frequent during the day, such as stores, schools, or airports.

Recently, I was in a department store in a checkout line, and in front of me was an African American woman. She barely got the credit card out of her wallet when the clerk told her, "I'll need to see your ID with that." She quickly produced her ID and handed it to the clerk, who took a good thirty seconds comparing it to her, her eyes skeptically darting back and forth between the picture and the woman. She finally returned the woman's ID, and silently dismissed her.

At first, I assumed the clerk was just adhering to policy, or possibly at the end of a very long shift. But when she turned to me to ring up my order, her face lightened and with a big friendly smile she asked, "Did you find everything you need?" She proceeded to check out my items quickly and efficiently, and when I handed her my credit card, I waited, and she never asked for my ID. So, getting the picture here, I said, "Don't you need to see my ID?" and she said, "No, it's OK." Incredulous, I took my ID out of my wallet and handed it to her anyway. I said, "Well, you asked for the ID of the woman before me, so that must be the policy here." She shrugged, barely glanced at my ID, and sent me on my way with a cheery, "Have a nice day!"

This is a minor example of how despite presumably legally equitable store policies, social practices can discriminate against people with non-dominant identities. Do we mindfully notice these practices? Do we mindfully challenge them? If we don't challenge them, they will continue to maintain an unfair system.

A few other subtle, nonviolent but insidious examples stem from the Christian-normative society we live in that tends to privilege and include some, and exclude others. Historically, those who don't celebrate Christmas are yearly subjected to Christmas music and decorations in what are supposed to be non-religious environments: the grocery store, the department stores, the doctor's office, the dentist's office, among others. I get it, the U.S. is a Christian nation. Last year on December 21st, I attended a yoga class for winter solstice. It also happened to be Chanukah. The yoga instructor came in and excitedly asked, "So who's ready for Christmas?" Of all places!

This December, on Chanukah, I went into a very well-known, large department store to find some Chanukah wrapping paper. As I entered the store, they had a big display of Christmas wrapping paper, on sale for $1 per roll. I searched through the cases and cases of rolls and found they were all covered in Christmas decorations. I went all the way back to where they usually carried wrapping paper, and still couldn't find any Chanukah paper. I asked a store clerk to help me. She told me all the Chanukah stuff was on the very end of an aisle in a tiny section, which she led me to. The wrapping paper was $7 per roll. I turned to her and said, "Wow, how is it that the Christmas paper is only $1 per roll at the front of the store, but the Chanukah paper is so expensive?" She looked at me and said, "Well, Christmas is around the corner so it's on sale." And I said, "But Chanukah is *today*!" As she shrugged, I took a deep breath, and met her eyes and said, "You do see the problem, don't you?" And as she started to shrug again, she paused, met my eyes with her own, and nodded, "Yes, I do."

This Christian-normative privilege is an institutionalized practice. This clerk did not make the policy. The most I could do is to bring this to the attention of the manager of the store, who in my experience of doing so would tell me, "Well, I don't set the prices, that's just store policy." And I could have written a letter to the corporation, which in my experience of doing so would result in a letter back thanking me for contacting them. On that day, I felt that mindfully connecting with the store clerk could make a difference, so that's what I chose to do.

It goes deeper when we think about our educational institutions. Last spring, I attended a session for teachers at the National Conference on Race and Ethnicity. The session was led by social justice groundbreaker and my colleague and friend, Dr. Eddie Moore, Jr. The session was filled mostly with administrators of K12 schools. After the inspirational and challenging presentation, one school principal raised her hand. When prompted, she said, "Well, I have good teachers in my school; they just don't get this diversity stuff." Eddie could have jumped in and talked about how to bring these conversations into the school system in an engaging, inviting way. Instead, he challenged the premise of the question.

He looked right at the woman who had spoken and said, "If they don't get this diversity stuff," then why do you say they are 'good teachers'?" He was asking all of us to rethink what we've been taught it means to be a "good teacher." If teachers are not incorporating culturally inclusive practices (not just around race, but also gender, sexuality, social class, disability, among others), they are not reaching all students. They are teaching only to students of the dominant culture, and perpetuating a system that includes some students at the expense of others. They are also sending a message to all students that this is the way things should be done.

How does this play out in the classroom? One way is demonstrated by GLSEN's (Gay, Lesbian, and Straight Education Network) annual national overview of the state of LGBTQ issues in K12 schools. In their most recent report, they found that 85% of LGBTQ students have experienced verbal harassment based on their perceived sexuality or gender expression, and 66% experienced LGBTQ-related discrimination. Worse yet, roughly 60% have heard homophobic and transphobic remarks from school staff.

When we know that LGBTQ adolescents are four times more likely to commit suicide than their heterosexual classmates, this behavior, from school staff especially, is not inconsequential. This creates a hostile environment for LGBTQ students and it's so bad that almost a third (32%) miss at least one day of school every month. Our supposed sacred educational system is not unbiased. Consider the ramifications of missing school – the decreased chances of success, and the increased likelihood of getting into trouble, among others.

How do we mindfully challenge our educational systems? Dr. Moore provided one way. He put the premise of the comment from the school administrator under scrutiny. He asked us all to mindfully reflect on our basic understanding of what it means to be a good teacher. I can guarantee that all of the school administrators in that room took this challenge seriously.

There are so many other institutions in U.S. society and beyond that have discrimination built into the way they do business. It is beyond the purview of this book to list them all. I am suggesting you mindfully pay attention and notice, notice, notice where and how systemic inequities play out on a daily basis in your home, schools, workplaces, stores, in the legal system, and the list goes on. Who is being followed around in the stores you frequent? Who isn't? Who is being pulled over for DWB (Driving While Black)? Who isn't? Who runs the Fortune 500 companies? Who doesn't? Who is in the boardrooms? Who isn't?

Privilege and discrimination are pervasive whether or not we notice them. As the late social justice author, activist, educator, and friend, Allan

Johnson said in his seminal book, *Privilege, Power, and Difference*, we have a choice in every single interaction: to become part of the problem or part of the solution. We must make the invisible, visible. In fact, I remember many years ago when Allan came to speak in my classroom at the university. He was giving a talk on campus and managed to squeeze in a visit with my students. He asked them, "What would happen if we did nothing about these inequalities?" Most of my students, who had just started reading his book, responded, "Nothing."

He spent most of the rest of the time he was with us countering their response with a strong evidence-based argument on how in actuality, if we do nothing, things will continue to get much worse. He provided statistics on discrimination in all of our institutions (housing, jobs, education, among others) off the top of his head, and talked about how doing nothing in effect perpetuates a hostile environment because it allows unfair treatment to continue, making life even better for some, and even harder for others. Doing nothing has consequences. Inaction harms; mindful action helps. It's our choice.

MINDFULLY BECOMING A SOCIAL JUSTICE ALLY/ADVOCATE

Using our Observer, we can mindfully witness the ways in which our privileges operate in our lives. When noticing the consequences of an egoic, oppressive, conditioned social system, we can either get angry or we can take action. Consider *ally* as a verb: to ally ourselves with others. If you are already an advocate for social justice and are well versed in how to speak up, I encourage you to come to the following suggestions with Beginner's Mind. Perhaps there is something here that can add to your already existing practice of taking action.

How can we use mindfulness to challenge systems of inequality? One way to begin is to make the decision to become a voice for change, or to further develop your voice.

MINDFULNESS PRACTICE 22
Choosing to Make a Difference

Get comfortable in a seated position. Breathe. With your eyes closed or gazed down, focus on your inhales and exhales. Let go of any distractions that come into your awareness.

Focus for a moment on all of the ways in which inequities and "fear of

Otherness" are fundamental aspects of this society. Consider how some people are made to feel included and like they belong in most places they go, and others are systematically excluded, made to feel like outsiders. Consider the consequences of these messages for all of us, how we benefit in some ways, based on certain social identities, and how we lose, based on other social identities.

Breathe in compassion and lovingkindness for the toll it takes on all of us to live in an unfair system. As you do so, make a promise that you will make a difference in this area. Your actions can contribute to a more compassionate, equitable world. What's at stake is the potential for a full, expansive, enriching life.

What intention can you set to make a difference? Sit with that question for a bit and see if your Inspired Self has a suggestion. Perhaps you can set the intention of speaking out against homophobia when you see it. Or learning how to become a better advocate for the homeless. Or choosing to get involved in the activism in your community around police brutality. Consider some options.

Maybe there is something you have been meaning to do, and right now, to live your best life, you make the commitment to figure out how to make it happen. Or you make the commitment to do the research on this social issue. Or maybe you have no idea what direction to go in but you know you want to do something. As you continue to ask the question, "What intention can I set?", ideas and opportunities will begin to arise.

When you're ready, take another deep breath, and flutter your eyes open. Stretch your body and take a moment to transition your focus back into the room.

Welcome back.

Feel free to journal now about your experience, or about any ideas or insights that arose for you.

As Maya Angelou said, "We come as one; we stand as 10,000." We do not come to this work of making a difference by ourselves, in a vacuum. You can ask yourself: With whom do I stand? Or you can ask: Who do I know in my life whose actions have made a difference in the area of social justice? What characteristics do/did they embody? How can I draw on their strength, and their example, as I move forward? Perhaps you can allow them to empower you to take action. They stand with you.

How can you fulfill your promise to mindfully make a difference? You can use your mindfulness practices as a tool to:

1. Focus on this present moment (what qualities/gifts do I have to contribute?).

2. Become a keen observer (what needs to be done?).

3. Use your Inspired Self to set an intention for taking action (what can I do?).

You have already answered the first question with Mindfulness Practice #5, "Finding your Gifts" in Chapter 1, "Social Conditioning – Living from the Outside In." The answer to the second question requires paying close attention to the social injustices that are pervasive in this society, and moving in the direction of any issue that speaks to you – that draws you in. And third, set an intention to follow that path, and allow yourself to see where that journey will take you. In this way, you can become an advocate for change by standing up for yourself and for those whose voices have been systematically silenced in this culture.

Whether you came up with some ideas in your meditation or not, the following are some other suggestions for mindfully take action.

You can set an intention to:

1. Learn more about what you don't know you don't know. Choose a social identity you don't know much about and learn about the culture before getting involved with people from it – do your homework.

2. Read multicultural books, do research, watch movies, attend multicultural events to learn more.

3. Research and join an organization that fights for the rights of people from traditionally marginalized social groups, and see how you can get involved.

4. Seek out ways to assertively, yet compassionately, challenge behavior, policies, organizations, or corporations that are exclusionary: those that include some and exclude others.

5. Take a course or training on how to become a social justice advocate.

6. Once you have background knowledge and the skills required to teach, find ways to become a resource for organizations and especially schools to help them become more culturally inclusive.

7. Get involved in the political system: vote for candidates who take action on issues of social justice and civil rights, work for these candidates, get

out the vote, host a house party, lobby your representatives along these issues; better still, run for office yourself.

8. Gather a group of people/neighbors/friends/family to discuss the topic of privilege or social justice and brainstorm ideas for making a difference (you can even start with a movie night and present a film on these issues that you can discuss after watching it, and then challenge them to consider how they can make a difference).

9. Think local: consider how you can be an agent of change in the communities you are already a part of (workspaces, family, religious/spiritual spaces).

10. Commit to being a voice for change every day.

Remember, it takes a community to work toward social justice. It is best to engage in this work in conversation, community action, and by building relationships across social differences: quite literally creating beloved community.

MINDFUL ACTION INVENTORY

Here's your opportunity to make a list of all the ways you personally can make a difference. Whether or not you are an experienced social justice advocate, we all have the capacity to increase our impact. Feel free to start your list with what came out of your meditation or by choosing from the list above, and then; get creative. Consider your own life, what you bring to the table, what needs to be done that is calling to you, and what you can do.

Once you are done with your list, go ahead and rank the list from least risky to most risky. Then, as Allan Johnson suggests, start with the least risky thing you can do, and when you get more and more experienced, you can make your way down the list to the most risky. Keep in mind that the list must never end. This is a lifelong process. You can add to it every time you think of a new way to make a difference.

In Judaism, the concept of Tikkun Olam, translated as "repairing the world," means we have an obligation to leave the world in better shape than it was before we got here.

Taking mindful action against biased systems in society is one way of doing just that. How will you make a difference? How will you use your voice, your vote, and your dollar, to transform the world and make it a place you and future generations would be proud to be a part of? This is one more way of developing an inspired life filled with meaning and purpose.

CHAPTER 12

Mindfully Connecting Social Justice & Environmental Justice

"We live in an interconnected world, in an interconnected time, and we need holistic solutions. We have a crisis of inequality, and we need climate solutions that solve that crisis." ~Naomi Klein

I used to pay little to no attention to the bumper sticker plea to "Save the Planet." I figured it was up to the scientists to figure out how to do that. Besides, I had enough to worry about focusing on advocating for human beings and civil rights. I knew humans had contributed to climate change, but the problem was too big for me to deal with, and I figured if I was recycling, I was doing my part.

It wasn't until I heard a lecture by Dr. Heather Hackman on how environmental justice is a social justice issue that I started to pay closer attention. She provided evidence to demonstrate how hurting the planet was really hurting the people on it. And who would be hurt first and worst by global warming? Who has insurance and who doesn't? These were questions I had never thought to ask.

Now when I bring up the topic of environmental justice in leading-edge social justice circles, they say the same thing to me: I don't really care about the planet; I'm more concerned with human beings. But what about the dispro-portionate effects of Hurricane Katrina on people of color and poor individu-als? What about the salmon disappearing in Alaska leaving Indigenous peoples without food staples? And there are so many more examples of how climate change is a social justice issue. As I learned more about the connections, I realized I had no choice but to continue to bring environmental justice into the conversation when I talk about mindfulness and social justice.

MINDFULNESS FOR ENVIRONMENTAL JUSTICE

First and foremost, when we think about transforming the world, environmental justice must be seminal to the discussion. Mindfulness allows us to pause and pay attention to our relationship to the planet, and see ourselves as interconnected with it. For example, take a look around the space you are currently in. Every single item you see, in its barest form, has come from the Earth: the food we eat, the fabric for the clothes we are wearing, the wood from the furniture in the room, the petroleum in the plastic travel mug holding our coffee, etc. When we practice mindfulness, we can pay attention to that connection and deeply honor it. The act of mindfulness transforms our relationship to each of these items, creating a connection that allows us to consider what we consume, how much we consume, how we treat the planet, and perhaps what we might do differently so that the planet can thrive for future generations.

All of this is intertwined, too, with food justice. In general, the more food we eat that comes most directly from the earth (not over-processed), the healthier it is, and the healthier we are. The earth provides exactly what we need for a healthy diet. Because of Conditioned Self, and a conditioned sense of greed, we have an overproduced meat industry. The methane produced from cows is contributing significantly to global warming, as are transportation emissions during the distribution process. The cattle require an immense amount of resources: water, corn, and other elements that deprive humans of farming areas that could otherwise be used for human consumption. According to the USDA, 41 million people in the U.S. live in households that do not have enough food. This means that there are human beings who are going hungry in the U.S., while cows are overfed so they can be sold and turned into more beef. This fact alone makes environmental justice a social justice issue, and once I realized that, I stopped eating factory-farmed meat.

Conditioned Self makes us believe that the planet and everything on it is ours, and that we can do whatever we want to it. Our relationship to the planet then becomes one of dominance and control. The westernized world's ideologies and practices, embedded in Conditioned Self, have become a culture of exploitation that is so normalized that we don't even recognize the fatal impact we are having. We are all implicated by the destruction.

Fighting for environmental justice means boycotting corporations that are poisoning water supplies that primarily affect impoverished communities of color. It means taking action against meat and corn industries that continue to destroy forests for cheap hamburgers and over-processed sugary products. Priced so low, they are the only food people in poverty can afford to eat, while fresh, organic vegetables are a luxury, consumed primarily by wealthy white people trying to slim down. This is what injustice looks like.

To live a sustainable, meaningful way of life, the Huichols and other Indigenous peoples ask the question: "What have we forgotten?" Overpowering Conditioned Self has forced us to forget. What we have forgotten is that we come from agricultural communities that engaged in practices that were rooted in the knowledge and understanding that the earth is sacred, humanity is sacred, and our lives and standards of living are inextricably linked to one another: that we are interconnected.

CONNECTING THE DOTS

Mindfulness practices allow us to connect inward to our Inspired Self for our own health and wellbeing, and for finding and actualizing our higher purpose in life. These practices also allow us to connect outward to other people to build deep, authentic relationships, especially across our differences, and to observe and challenge systemic, institutionalized inequities. Mindfulness can also provide a means for deeply connecting outward to the planet on which we live.

I like to think of it this way:

- If we mindfully cherish ourselves, we will manifest our best life. We will treat ourselves well and are more likely to take care of ourselves physically, emotionally, and even spiritually.
- If we mindfully cherish other people, we will create relationships that are exceedingly meaningful, supportive, and joyful, which will increase our sense of belonging. When we get to know, and appreciate people who have a different social group membership than our own, we are less likely to discriminate against that group, and are more likely to advocate for that group. This is social justice.
- If we mindfully cherish the planet, we are less likely to harm it with pollution of any kind, and we are more likely to advocate by fighting climate change. This is environmental justice.

Connecting the dots between mindfulness, social justice, and environmental justice, we can create a sustainable way of life. The following mindfulness practice brings these ideas together to clarify their, and our, interconnectedness.

MINDFULNESS PRACTICE 23
Interconnectedness

Please find a comfortable seated position, if that works on your body. Feel the weight of yourself in your seat. If your feet are touching the floor, ground yourself down into the floor by paying attention to how your feet feel and the stability of the ground beneath your feet. Feel how your back touches the back of your chair. If it is available to you, see if you can lengthen your spine just a little by lifting the crown of your head toward the ceiling. And breathe deeply.

Feel free to close your eyes or gaze down as you pay special attention to the inhales and exhales of your body. On the inhale, notice as your body fills up with air, focusing on any area that feels strained or tense, and on the exhale, see if you can release any stress or tension in your body. Let it go.

Take a few rounds of breath at your own inhale/exhale pace. Keep in mind that your breath is always a constant in your life. It will be with you every moment you are alive. Focusing on it at any time has a way of centering or grounding us in the present moment and in what is. Our breath can also provide insight into how we are managing the world around us. Is your breath smooth? Jagged? Fast? Slow? Just noticing the quality of our breath can broaden our perspective and can calm our parasympathetic system. It is difficult, if not impossible, to breathe deeply and be stressed at the same time.

Notice, too, your connection to the earth. Whether it is your feet that are touching the earth or the legs of your chair or the wheels of your wheelchair, feel the energy from the earth grounding you. Although we are sitting on the surface of the earth, and although the earth is moving, when we connect to it, we are of it. It feels solid beneath us. Know that it is also a constant in our lives.

Consider again the earth on which we sit. Whose land are we on? Before it was colonized, which peoples lived on it? What might their communities have looked like? Can you imagine their faces? What might their lives have been like? How might our world and our ways of knowing be different without our history of colonization? Take another deep breath in, connecting your breath with those people whose faces you imagined. We are all interconnected.

When you are ready, if your eyes are closed, flutter them open. Find an item in the room to gaze at. It can be anything: a chair, a picture, a glass of water, a light switch, anything. Focus on this item. Consider its shape, size, and color. Is it smooth or bumpy? Round or square? Hard or soft? Now consider that at its basic core, it was made from some element that originated in the earth. Focus on where it might have come from: where its life began. Breathe into its essence.

Consider the way the element was mined. Think about the metal machines that dug into or under the surface of the earth for the sole purpose of creating this item or other items like it. Think about the exhaust that comes from those machines and the potential impact on human breath and on the earth's ozone layer and the resulting greenhouse effects.

Consider this item's journey. How did it become what it is? How likely is it that this item was made in this country? Where in the world did the item come from? Whose hands have touched this item along the way not only to manufacture it, but also to transport it here into this room? How likely is it that those hands were brown-skinned?

Think about the person those hands belong to: Is the person working in a factory? Have they been given a safety mask to protect them from toxic chemicals? Has health insurance been provided to them in case of injuries such as asthma, heart conditions, or accidents such as the loss of a limb? Were they paid a fair wage for their labor, and was their paycheck enough to provide food for their family?

Focus once again on your own breath. Imagine now connecting your breath with the breath of the people who have manufactured, transported, touched this item in some way. Breathe, taking all of that in. We are interconnected.

Slowly focus your attention back to your own body. Contemplate all the millions of items we come across, consume, and throw away every day. How would our health, our relationships, and our world be different if we practiced this short mindfulness technique when we came in contact with items throughout our day? Would it make a difference in terms of what we chose to purchase or consume?

When you are ready, take another deep breath. Stretch your body and take a moment to transition your focus back into the room.

Welcome back.

Feel free to journal now about your experience, or about any ideas or insights that arose for you.

We have been taught not to notice or acknowledge the reality that we are all connected. At a time when our planet is heating up at an alarming pace, this reflection is not inconsequential. Mindfulness practices can transform the ways in which we see, relate to, and honor ourselves, each other, and the planet.

ACKNOWLEDGING INTERCONNECTEDNESS

There are many ways to stay aware of our interconnectedness. Many people find that sense through nature. Being outdoors connects us with something much larger than ourselves. Just looking up at the sky can bring about a sense of unity with all other beings on the planet who are also looking up at the sky, or just living their lives under it. I would consider spending time outdoors a best practice, too, for environmental justice. We need to remember, and keep in the forefront of our consciousness, what we are advocating for. If we stay inside all the time, it is a bigger leap toward understanding why it is important to connect with and protect the planet.

We can bring our connection to the planet into every breath we take. We can mindfully focus on the fact that with every single inhale, we are receiving the oxygen we need to survive and thrive directly from the trees, and with every exhale, we are expelling carbon dioxide, providing the trees exactly what they need to survive and thrive. It is a perfect symbiosis and reminds us of our direct connection to the planet: it is a source of energy for us, as we are to it. We are not separate from it, ever. If we are alive, we are connected to the earth. And even after we die, our physical body can remain connected to the planet. What if we considered our connection to the earth at any time of the day we're feeling disconnected, in fear, or in stress? How might changing our awareness influence our mindset, or our sense of peace? How might it change our behavior toward, or gratitude for, the planet?

Another mindful practice for environmental justice is to create and engage in beloved community. One way to do this is to join and spend time with people outside of your household who have a common sense of purpose – preferably fighting for something you believe in like social justice or some aspect of the planet. This kind of connection provides a sense of belongingness, shared meaning, and a greater sense of the world. This can also be achieved by traveling to other countries, if that is available to you. A firsthand experience getting outside your own home or neighborhood can provide valuable perspective, and brings home the message that even in light of our cultural differences, all human beings around the planet have a shared humanity.

CURBING CONSUMPTION

Recycling can be considered a mindfulness practice for environmental justice in that each and every time we pause to consider if an item can be recycled, and walk to the recycle bin rather than to the landfill bin, we are connecting to the planet. Recycling, however, will not save the Earth. Instead we must think much bigger. Today, our greatest asset in lowering both our negative impact on the earth, and our carbon footprint, is ingenuity. We need every person to ask: What kind of energy am I using up; what waste am I leaving behind; and what is my impact on the planet?

Consider that plastic containers are made up of a limited earthly resource: petroleum. I invite you into your own bathroom. Look around. It is likely that most of the products you have purchased: your shampoos, conditioners, lotions, creams, gels, and whatever other products you use, are held in containers made of plastic. Now think about the billions of other bathrooms just like yours.

And this doesn't even broach the idea of bottled water. Many places, such as Colorado, have extremely fresh water, yet consumers are still prompted, conditioned, sold on the idea that they need to buy bottled water instead of just turning on the tap. Bottled water is sold in bottles which take roughly three times the water to produce the water inside them. While some people do not have access to clean water and must buy it bottled, the vast majority of those who buy it have access to clean water from the tap.

This is consumerism at its worst. I mention this not to provoke feelings of guilt or shame, but rather to notice that Conditioned Self has an incredible impact. The marketing of bottled water has worked well and tapped into our desire for convenience at the expense of scarce resources such as the oil and water it takes to make the bottles. The good news is we can take mindful action!

We can set an intention to lower our own personal carbon footprint. In this way, we become part of the solution, rather than further contributing to the problem. We can set an intention to take the time to consider our consumption patterns, and reflect on how they are interconnected with the Earth. We can consider carrying around a reusable stainless steel or glass water bottle and refilling it throughout our day. We can bring a mug or thermos with us to the coffeehouse. We can ask ourselves with every purchase: Is this a *want* or a *need*? If we focus on consuming more needs than wants, we are already headed in a direction that demonstrates our connection with, and desire to heal, the planet. What if everyone asked this question with every purchase? That alone would lower our overall consumption, and subsequently, the damage to the earth caused by overproduction.

Thich Nhat Hanh teaches a beautiful moving meditation that asks us to consider our actual footprints (or wheelprints) on the ground. This medita-tion is best done in motion: gliding forward as we contemplate our impact on the planet. It can be done inside or outside – whichever feels better and/or is available to you.

MINDFULNESS PRACTICE 24
Impact on the Earth

If it is available to you to engage in this mindfulness practice as a walking meditation, please first stand in one place, take a deep breath, and come into this present moment. If you are seated, pause, breathe, and come into this present moment. As you exhale, feel your connection to the planet beneath you. Can you feel where your body ends and the earth below you begins? Breathe some love into that imagined space. Notice how your body feels in this moment, on this earth. Notice the stillness in the moment – in not moving.

When you are ready, slowly move forward, paying close attention to your movement. Consider what it takes in your mind and body to go from stationary to moving forward. Feel your muscles engage. Pay special attention to your connection to the earth. If you are walking, feel each foot rise and gently place it down in front of you. Notice how as your foot gets planted on the earth, the rest of your body's weight shifts forward as your other foot comes off the ground. If you are in a wheelchair, notice the movement forward and the connection to the earth between the wheels and the ground.

Continue to slowly move forward, using your Observer to notice your movements, and also find yourself in your body, noticing how each movement forward feels. We rarely take the time to notice how our body moves. See if you can find a connection or rhythm between your breath and your movement. Perhaps one step could be an inhale and the next could be an exhale. Or even slow it down more, taking a full inhale and exhale with each step.

As you move forward, if you are outside, or are near a window, see if you can mindfully soak in your surroundings, breathing in the fresh air, appreciat-ing the earth on which we live. Then, consider, as Thich Nhat Hanh suggests, how we move forward in the world. How gently do we go? Are we trampling the earth, or treading lightly? And as we move forward, consider what we are leaving behind with every step? As we connect our carbon footprint to our actual footprints or wheelprints, we can ask ourselves: what is my impact on the earth? We have a choice in every move we make.

What if we were to mindfully proceed through our lives from our Inspired

Self, making a deep impact on others but little to no impact on the planet? What would that look like for you? What might you have to change in your life for that to be so? What might the cumulative impact be on the planet if every person were to live this way?

When you are ready, come to a stationary position. Pause, and again, notice the difference in your body from moving forward to becoming stationary. Notice your connection to the earth now. Take another deep breath. Stretch your body and take a moment to transition your focus back into your surroundings.

Welcome back.

Feel free to journal now about your experience, or about any ideas or insights that arose for you.

Many of the practices in this book ask you to consider the world differently. Rather than moving through the world, and your life, mindlessly, it asks you to consider what your life and the world might be like to proceed mindfully, paying attention as you go. Again, this takes practice, and may not be something you can do every moment of every day, but that is not the point. The goal here is to remember your Inspired Self throughout your day as often as possible.

EMBODIMENT OF CONSUMPTION: FOOD JUSTICE

Our reduced impact on the earth is about minimizing our waste to lessen our carbon footprint, and it can also incorporate what we are physically ingesting. In the United States, the air we consume seems fresh, but it is becoming more and more toxic from overproduction and chemical waste. Consider what else we ingest. Our food intake is directly related to our connection to our bodies and to the earth.

Conditioned Self tells us that if something tastes good, we should have more of it. It is widely known now that large food producers spend a ton of resources to find the exact combination of ingredients (chemically enhanced, or just simply chemicals) that produce the best, but not most satisfying, taste. This creates the ideal conditions for consumers to want and buy more and more, which obviously is exactly the goal of the food producers.

What happens, however, when we eat more food than our bodies need? We can become lethargic. Our bodies then must work hard to digest all of the food we've ingested. We are also unlikely to be able to digest all of the chemically-processed foods on the shelves in the supermarket. We are becoming heavier, sicker, and less motivated to do anything about it. In short, we are doing a disservice to our sacred human form.

Dietary overconsumption/obesity has reached epidemic proportions in the United States. This is due, at least in part, to the overconsumption of processed foods rather than eating foods that are closer to their original form when they grow out of the earth. As author and educator Michael Pollan suggests, "Don't eat anything your great-grandmother wouldn't recognize as food." His popular dietary recommendation comes in the form of a 7-word haiku: *Eat food. Not too much. Mostly plants.* If half of your plate at every meal is filled with "plants" or some type of greens, you're probably doing pretty well in this arena. I think about a healthy diet as filling half the plate with greens, a quarter with protein, and a quarter with some type of carbohydrates.

Yet, who has access to plants? One aspect of social and environmental justice is food justice: who has access to healthy food and who doesn't? The places where people have little or no access to food (such as in rural areas) are known as food deserts, whereas the places where they only have access to convenience store foods with little to no fresh fruit and vegetables, in short, little to no nutrition, are known as food swamps. Food swamps are primarily situated in neighborhoods filled with people with lower socio-economic status and with black and brown skinned bodies. This is a systemic problem.

We can curb this problem with public gardens and by supporting local farms. What if every public flower garden was turned into an edible garden instead? Not only would we be minimizing hunger, we would be providing healthy food to nourish and sustain human beings. As stated by the urban farmer Ron Finley in his TedTalk, "A Guerilla Gardener in South Central L.A.," "When kids grow kale, kids eat kale." What if we taught kids to grow their own healthy food? How might that transform the way we engage neighborhoods, create healthy living, promote wellbeing, and just as importantly, a feeling of belongingness?

MINDFUL EATING

Mindful eating is another way to connect us to the food we eat. There are many books on this topic so I won't elaborate here. The important thing to note is that mindful eating allows more of our senses into the process of consuming our food. First, we can pause before eating, offering gratitude for the food before us. If it is available to us, we can mindfully look at the food and appreciate how it was prepared (mindful cooking is a whole other book!). We can mindfully breathe in the smell of the food and appreciate the nuances in the aromas. We can listen to any sound that emanates from the food (sizzling if it's hot; or the sound of our utensil as it touches our plate or bowl). All this, before we even begin to lift the food to our lips to taste it.

Thich Nhat Hanh recommends that every time we put food in our mouths, we spend even a few seconds imagining the food we are ingesting in its original form. So, if we are eating a piece of wheat bread, we can imagine the source of the bread: the wheat swaying in the wind. If we're eating a piece of fruit, we can imagine it before it was picked, perhaps imagining the raindrops that fell on it during its time on the tree or vine. We can imagine the sunlight shining on the lettuce we are ingesting, as it was growing in the garden. This is one way we can connect our lives and our bodies with the earth that sustains us.

As a reminder of the connection between the food I eat and what it represents on a larger scale in terms of my relationship to my body, other people in my life, and to the planet, I keep this list of affirmations on my refrigerator. It is a revised version of "5 Contemplations for Eating" created by Thich Nhat Hanh.

1. May we be aware that this food is a gift from the earth, the sky, the Universe, and the numerous living beings and much hard work that brought it to our table.
2. May we eat this food with mindfulness and gratitude so as to be worthy to receive it.
3. May this food nourish our bodies and provide *only* and exactly what we need to thrive.
4. May this food nurture our compassion so that we connect deeply with each other, strengthen our community, and reduce the suffering of all living beings.
5. May we thoroughly enjoy this food in a way that connects us deeply with the planet from where it came.

MINDFULNESS FOR HEALTH JUSTICE

One of my clients recently said to me, "I don't have time to meditate. All of my waking hours are filled with making sure I have food on the table and a roof over my head." The assumption that everyone has time to sit down for twenty minutes or more every single day is a privileged idea. Not everyone has the time to learn mindfulness practices, or the time to engage in them.

In fact, we could even ask, who has the privilege of buying and reading this book? Moreover, who has access to health and wellness strategies in general, and who doesn't? Who has health insurance that focuses not just on illness, but on wellness, and who doesn't? These are health justice questions.

One strategy to minimize the disparity in access to wellness is to know and share the idea that mindful practices can happen at any time of day, and even while you're doing other things. You can focus on your breath while you're waiting in line, or stopped at a red light, or sitting in traffic, or waiting for the bus, or even in the bathroom! Once acquainted with the practices, they are truly accessible to everyone at any time.

Among a myriad of documented health benefits, one of the best gifts mindfulness practices provide is to prepare us to respond (rather than react) to any situation mindfully, in alignment with your Inspired Self. When I first began to mindfully focus on my breath, over time, something started to shift within me. At first, I started out witnessing my breath, and inevitably, by focusing on it, it would slow down. I could feel my chest expand and contract, my belly soften, my shoulders relax. What I began to notice is that after several months of paying attention to this calming breath throughout my day, when I got into a stressful situation during the rest of my day, my calming breath would kick in automatically, and I would relax. This was so profound that there have been times where my brain didn't even recognize the situation as stressful until I realized my breath had changed – it had become slower and deeper. In other words, my body was calming me down first, before I even knew I needed to check in with my breath. The result is that I was more able to respond to the situation before me from a calm place, rather than getting more worked up about what was occurring. Consider the implications for this one practice in terms of how we show up in the world, how we interact, and even as a leadership practice.

THE SANCTUARY WITHIN

It is easy to say the problem of social, food, health, and environmental justice is too big and that we cannot possibly make a difference. I am not concerned, however, with the actions of the whole world; I am only interested in *your* actions. How do you feel in your own body? How do you feel in the world? How do you show up? Do you feel good about the choices you make?

In their book, *Active Hope*, ecophilosopher Dr. Joanna Macy and psychologist Dr. Chris Johnstone suggest we ask the question, "What happens through you?" This question invites us to consider what we are allowing to occur in the world, both the negative and the positive. How are our actions examples of being a voice for change? How and when do we speak up for voices who have been silenced? How are we being of service rather than sitting by and watching?

Mindfulness practices allow us the opportunity to get still and listen to our own Inner Knowing – to be proud of the actions we have taken already. The fact that you are still reading this book demonstrates a clear commitment to peace and justice, for yourself, for others, and for the planet. Our Inner Knowing, that place within that already knows, is our sanctuary. It is the place that can guide us to make decisions that come from love and empathy. Our sanctuary within.

Based on the practices provided in this chapter on mindful consumption, mindful eating, mindful movement, health/wellness, among others, I invite you to take a moment to write down some of the practices you might incorporate into your own life. As you do so, keep in mind that justice work is challenging, and lends itself to burnout. What mindfulness practices might you incorporate that will keep you healthy and inspired for the long haul?

CONCLUSION

Takeaways

Ubuntu means I am because we are.

A couple of weeks after my dearest friend, Daryl, to whom this book is dedicated, passed away from leukemia, I found myself living in two worlds. I was with him when he passed, having virtually moved in with him and his husband the few weeks prior, to spend time with him and to help him through his transition. It was one of the most profound experiences of my life. Based on our connection that was filled with intensely moving conversations, he knew I had access to both the spiritual and the physical world. I believe he needed me to walk with him in his journey because he knew I would not be afraid, and I might provide him with some company and comfort as he transitioned. I was honored to comply.

In the few weeks before his death, it was clear to me that I was being called to serve in this way. I knew it was holy work and that I was being asked to rise to the occasion and support him in any way I could. Although no one close to me had ever passed before, I did not hesitate.

Because he had accepted his fate, I did the same. I did not try to eke out one more day at any point, because I didn't want to see him, or his husband, suffer any more than necessary. And as much as I appreciated the gratitude his friends and loved ones kept offering me for what I was doing for Daryl, there wasn't a moment when I felt I could or would have wanted to be anywhere else but by his side. No thanks necessary.

When he passed, this beautiful soul, filled with love and light, let go of his earthly body. I was holding his hand, and I knew he was finally at peace.

In the weeks following his passing, I was granted what felt to me like an incredible state of grace. His husband and I cried and laughed, telling stories, immersed in the memory of Daryl's laughter and playful, beautiful, loving energy. At the same time, his warm energy lives within me, and I feel it constantly. It makes me smile.

Following Daryl's passing, the biggest challenge of the whole journey has been returning to what I perceive as the physical realm. I was living in a state of spiritual consciousness that I had never experienced quite so deeply before, and coming back to the physical reality of my life felt like being splashed with ice water on a cold winter's day. My Conditioned Self saw it as two realities: the spiritual and the physical, as a duality. As such, I felt like I had one toe in the Universe beyond, and the rest of my body was here on earth. Trying to wrap my brain around all of that was a ridiculous waste of time, and yet my Ego/Conditioned Self kept trying to make sense of it.

I am incredibly grateful for my mindfulness practices because they allowed me to simply be a witness to my experience. I have opened even more to the notion that perhaps there is no duality: as I mentioned at the beginning of this book, we are spiritual beings having a human experience. It is all a spiritual realm and we are currently inhabiting these bodies in what we perceive to be "real lives." Yet these real lives are inspired lives, whether we notice, perceive, believe, or experience them as such.

And as I navigate the healing process, I am doing my best to listen to my body for guidance. It knows exactly what it needs. I have allowed myself the grace to heal from weeks of hypervigilance of assessing Daryl's every shift in condition to make sure he was getting just what he needed at any given moment. I am back to teaching and speaking engagements, and writing. I show up in those spaces from my Inspired Self. Nothing less is worth my time or energy. I have also allowed myself the moments in between to simply reflect on all that I've been through, with amazement and gratitude.

Look, I don't pretend to have all the answers. I, too, am a product of my social conditioning. But when you strip away as much of the social conditioning as you can, we are left only with our Light and our Energy. For me, connecting to this is wonderful, and brings an enormous sense of peace, expansiveness, and wellbeing. And in these physical bodies we inhabit, we can only even conceive of that Light and Energy through the lens of these physical bodies. We can only use language to talk about these concepts through the intellect; our mind gives us the words, and our mouths allow those words to flow. We can only be in the Flow in the here and now – in this body – in this plane – on this green earth.

Coming so close to the experience of death, and witnessing the transition of my dear friend has certainly made me question whether or not there is, as I have written in this book, a higher purpose to our lives. This is a powerful question. And I admit that it's possible that there isn't one. Ultimately, however, the choice is ours to make. I only know from my own experience, that my life works much better when I believe in a higher purpose, and when I am connected to it, and live my life in alignment with it. My life takes on a much greater significance; it is a life filled with meaning.

Most people don't choose when they will die. And we don't know how long we will live in this body. So, it is important to ask the question: What will you do with your time here? How can you best make use of the time you do have? My choice is to live a life of purpose and meaning, to connect deeply with others (and the planet), to be of service as often as possible, and to find joy wherever and whenever I can.

Here are a few strategies, in no particular order, that have served me well, and I know will continue to be useful for me. In my daily meditation, these have been a few of the answers I have received when I have asked the question, "What do I need right now in this moment?" They have become mantras for me some days.

TAKEAWAYS FOR TAKING YOUR LIFE TO THE NEXT LEVEL

1. Love yourself – We spend so much time listening to the voice of Conditioned Self in our heads that we can neither see, acknowledge, nor appreciate the surface or depth of our beauty within. No matter how you feel about yourself or your body, at the very least, practice acknowledging anything (no matter how minor) that you appreciate about yourself. Where our thoughts go, energy flows. The more you acknowledge what you love, the more you will find to love.

2. Self-care – We (especially women) are taught to care for others first and foremost. There is nothing wrong with being of service. It can be the key to a fulfilling life. Being effective in this arena, especially for the long haul, however, absolutely necessitates finding ways to care for ourselves. As is said on a plane ride, when there's turbulence and the oxygen masks drop down from the roof of the plane, put yours on first before assisting others. Without finding your own "oxygen mask" first – you will become depleted, burned out, and ultimately, unable to care for or be of service to others. Find whatever serves you best to refuel, replenish, nurture, and heal you. Do that for at least a few minutes every single day, without fail.

3. Come from love – When we are in a stressed state, either from being overtired, overworked, or dealing with something profound, we are less likely to behave mindfully; we are more likely to react rather than respond. This plays out in our relationships with ourselves and in our relationships with others. We tend to overeat and make other bad choices; we tend to strike out against ourselves ("how could I be so …?") and against others ("how could you be so…?"). At these times, it is critically important to pause and breathe, and find compassion for yourself or for others. Try to come back to gratitude and if possible, from a place of love. It may take some time, but in my experience, it is always worth the wait. Every single time.

4. Expansion vs Contraction – When making a major or even a minor decision, always look for which choice brings you a feeling of expansion or light. That openness will lead you to more and more exciting opportunities. Doing what you "should" do is typically a contracted option. If you feel obligated, find a way to turn it around to come from a place of love, compassion, generosity, perhaps even hope. Ask yourself: Is there some underlying benefit to this option? Can I find any expansiveness in choosing this path? If there is none, then it is more likely that it is not a choice, but rather a requirement. Get it done quickly and efficiently, and move on to things that give you a feeling of expansiveness.

5. What do you need in this moment? This is a question that you can ask yourself on a daily basis, or in any moment where you are stuck or feeling challenged in any way. Ask yourself: What mindful meditation or mantra do I need right now? This, too, is self-care, and a service to yourself.

6. Practice Allowing – Most often, our suffering is caused by resistance to what is. When we experience suffering, it is because we refuse or are unable to accept what is – whether it is something that is occurring in our lives, or a challenging or disturbing emotion, feeling, experience, or thought. Our suffering is often rooted in the past (based on a story of how we were taught things were supposed to be), or in the future (how we were taught things are supposed to go). Once we can recognize that we are wishing that things were different than they are, then we can see that suffering is optional. What is called for is to practice the mindful art of allowing what is, to be just as it is. Acknowledge the frustration or sadness or whatever other emotion that comes up, and allow it to be. This does not mean we don't fight for justice or stand up for equity, but rather to allow, in this moment, what comes up for us to come up, and breathe through it. Know that whatever we are experiencing is temporary – even if the situation is a long-term issue, we can only experience it in the here and now – in this exact moment. Whatever ways you are suffering will likely pass, and pass quickly.

7. Moving from thinking to sensing/experiencing – What might life be like if we used our senses more? We tend to "think" things through rather than "feel" them through. There is nothing wrong with using our intellect to help guide us in our lives, but there is so much other knowledge we can gain from our bodies. We can ask ourselves: How does this idea or action resonate with me? How does it feel in my body? What kind of energy arises when I consider it? In my experience, when I use this knowledge, this way of knowing, and even prioritize it over my thinking mind, I tend to proceed with a much stronger sense of confidence, which makes it more likely that I will excel in that direction. Spirituality is opening your heart to experience the world from a sensing rather than an intellectual knowing, to use senses rather than thought to learn and grow and live.

8. Pull vs. push - Our actions often come from a place of pushing ourselves to do something. Although I got a lot done with a Type-A, no nonsense, "I mean business" kind of personality, I never felt satisfied with anything I got done. It was never enough. I was constantly pushing, pushing, pushing myself – and others. My mindfulness practices have provided me with a whole new perspective. I can push when I need to, but most often, I set an intention, trust in the process, let go of my attachment to the outcome, and follow the path I am drawn or pulled toward. I have found so much more peace and contentment this way, and what I have created in my life instead, has been beyond what I ever dreamed possible for myself.

9. I am a soul and when I see you as a soul, I treat you as such – Our social conditioning forces us to see each other as superficial beings; we interact with others on a surface level. Again, use whatever language resonates with you here. Consider what it might mean to see yourself as a sacred being? How might you treat yourself differently? What if each person you came into contact with was also sacred? How would you treat them? The idea is that if we are, in fact, spiritual beings in these human bodies, then we are all sacred/light/love/energy/etc. What if we treated each other as such? My closing offering in every yoga class is: May we awaken to the sacredness in ourselves, in each other, and in the planet.

10. Both/And mentality – We often see ourselves as living as/coming from either Conditioned Self or as Inspired Self. In actuality, in this physical plane, we are more than both. Our challenge and practice is to see ourselves as greater than the sum of these two aspects of ourselves as often as possible. Remember that in order to focus on our breath, we need both a mind to focus and a body to be aware of. To realize our potential in this world and on this planet, we need a physical egoic self to move through the world making decisions, building relationships, and to tap into our Inner Knowledge, our conscious awareness, our personal guidance system. We need all of it!

YOU ARE RIGHT ON TIME

We live our lives in such a rush. How much can we get done in a day? This is our culture. This is Conditioned Self. Through mindfulness practices, as you shift to come from Inspired Self as often as possible, know that you are right on time. What I learned from my grieving process is not to try to rush it. After about a month, I found myself thinking: "OK, it's time to move on; I've got stuff to do." Or I asked myself: "Why am I not through this yet?" For anyone who has grieved the transition of a loved one, you may recognize this pressure and realize how ridiculous it is to believe we can rush these things. My mindfulness practice reminded me to be exactly where I am. As soon as I paused and accepted where I was, my healing ironically seemed to speed up!

As you move forward in your own mindfulness practice, I encourage you to accept where you are. You are coming to, or developing, your mindfulness practice at exactly the time and pace you need to. No need to push yourself or compare your progress with anyone else. This is your practice. This is your time.

I conclude with one final mindfulness practice that asks you to consider what would have to shift in your life to live your own "heaven" on earth, today?

MINDFULNESS PRACTICE 25
Living an Inspired Life

Get comfortable in a seated position. Breathe. With your eyes closed or gazed down, focus on your inhales and exhales. On your exhale, let go of any distractions that come into your awareness.

When you are ready, consider how you want to feel in your life, as much or as often as possible. Happy? Joyful? Open? Expansive? Inspired? Whatever you choose, breathe in that feeling. Know that that exact feeling is only one breath away at any given moment of your day. Continue to breathe that feeling into your body for as long as you like.

When you are ready, consider how you want to be in your life, as much or as often as possible. How do you want to show up as you interact with others? Not how do you want them to see you, but rather, how do you want to show up in other people's presence? Open? Present? Welcoming? With a smile? Whatever you choose, breathe in that exact feeling. As you exhale, immerse yourself in that state of being. Your mindfulness practice can be as simple as remembering this feeling anytime you interact, or preferably before you interact with another living being.

When you are ready, consider what you would like to do in your life. If there is such a thing as having a purpose, or purposes, in your life, what would you like to use your gifts for? What would it feel like to be using your gifts more often, perhaps to be of service to one or many people? Breathe in that exact feeling. Know that you have access to that option, that purpose, and that feeling at any time during your day.

When you are ready, ask yourself: What can I shift in my life to use my gifts more often? What can I do to infuse my life with more meaning? What action can I take today to head in that exact direction? What am I open to? What is waiting to emerge?

When you are ready, take another deep breath, and flutter your eyes open. Stretch your body and take a moment to transition your focus back into the room.

Welcome back.

Feel free to journal now about your experience, or about any ideas or insights that arose for you.

All of this is only one breath away. All it takes is remembering it's available to you.

REFLECTING ON OUR SHARED FUTURE

When I was dealing with my own trauma, my biggest fear was the damage it would cause my children. I was afraid because I had spent two years of my childhood with a mother who was struggling every day to get out of bed, and to stay alive. I did not want to pass that experience on to my children. Unhealed trauma, however, does not live in a vacuum. We do not get to choose whether or not the young people in our lives will be affected by our own actions: know that they will.

At the height of dealing with my trauma, my daughter, Rachel developed a digestive disorder. In the midst of my own post-traumatic stress reaction, I made a plethora of doctor's appointments, and held her hand as she was subjected to every test imaginable, in the hopes that they could figure out what was causing her such discomfort and pain. They never could. In my heart, I believed, and still do, that the experience of losing the mom she had always known, and realizing there was nothing she could do to bring me back, was so unbearable to her that disease formed in her belly.

I am in no way suggesting she caused her own pain; quite the contrary. Intergenerational trauma is a well-researched field of study that demonstrates the connection between past experiences and present circumstances. Healing is called for. The work I did to overcome the bulk of my trauma has also affected Rachel for the better. What has grown between us in place of what was, is a profound new relationship grounded in mindfulness and deep spiritual connection. When we as a society consider our shared future: What are we creating today to help or hurt the future of humanity and the planet? What impact are we making?

MINDFUL, INCLUSIVE LEADERSHIP

What might our shared future look like for organizations and institutions if they were to incorporate mindfulness practices? How might that affect the way we "do business" in our society? The great news is this is already happening. More and more corporations and organizations are choosing to operate more consciously, and to identify as "conscious businesses." Given a seal of approval from B Lab (a non-partisan, nonprofit organization that rates for-profit businesses on social, organizational, and environmental criteria), they are referred to as triple-bottom line companies: attending to profit, person, and planet.

Beyond focusing only on the company's revenue (profit), these corporations pay attention to each employee's needs and even desires (person). They care about the health and wellbeing of each employee, personal empowerment, and helping them uncover and work towards their life's purpose to live a meaningful life. Studies have found this increases morale, productivity, and in fact, lowers sick days, which saves the corporations millions of dollars every year. Focusing on the person also refers to developing a diversity and inclusion strategic plan so that every member feels like they belong.

Research shows that organizations that include diversity and cultural inclusion in their policies and plans fare much better than those that do not.

The third bottom-line is a focus on our connection to the earth (planet). These companies research and develop sustainable practices because they take into account their impact on the earth for future generations. Some of the companies that are not only succeeding but soaring using this model are: Seventh Generation, Method Home, DHL, Patagonia, among others. More will follow suit if we demand that they do.

We are on the precipice of a new frontier. It will take mindful leadership that highlights inclusive excellence to leave the planet and its inhabitants in better shape than it was when we got here. It will take mindful leaders:

- who know to *respond* rather than to *react* to any given situation;
- who excel at mindful listening by using Beginner's Mind to hear and appreciate new and different voices than have been traditionally allowed to speak;
- and who operate in mindful awareness of our impact on the earth.

What would it mean for your life to allow yourself to be guided by your Inner Knowing? What if every leader (including you) did so? Consider how we might ascend together. What if every leader mindfully considered, as Indigenous tribes suggest, we make every decision based on the needs of seven generations in the future? What kind of world would we live in, then?

Using the mindfulness practices shared in this book, and other practices we find on our journeys, we can make a practice plan to a live a transformed life of increased health and wellbeing. And we can be a conduit of transformation for others in the ways we show up and interact. From our divine spark, we can innovate new systems that are more equitable. How might we envision a beloved future where we hold each other as sacred, and are responsible for and to each other? We are here together; we have a shared future. What do you hope your life and the world will look like in 10 years? What will be your contribution? What needs to shift to make that happen?

Wayne Dyer taught that we have but two options at every step in our life's journey: to either plug ourselves into/connect with our expanded awareness at any given moment, or not to. When we choose to access that energy, we are living an Inspired life. We can then bring our whole selves into the room, and invite others to do the same. No need to leave any part of our identity, our heart, or sense of self, at the door. We feel welcome, and welcome others. This lays the ground for excellence and innovation to occur. We can intentionally create these kinds of spaces in every place we find ourselves.

You are in a position, no matter what you do in life, to make mindful choices about yourself, your life, and the world. You always have access to living an Inspired Life. May you take advantage of the opportunity and use it well.

You have lots of options to take your life and/or your organization to the next level:

- Download or stream all 25 mindfulness practices offered in *The Mindfulness Effect* for FREE!

- Get *The Mindfulness Effect Journal & Practice Planner* to move your life forward;

- Join The Mindfulness Effect Facebook Community to connect with others about your mindfulness journey: ask questions, receive guidance, share experiences, and learn more;

- Sign up for The Mindfulness Effect Online Course to deepen your practice and gain further insight from the author;

- Sign up for our newsletter and blogs;

- Learn more about the services Dena Samuels Consulting offers (mindfulness-based diversity, equity, and inclusion keynotes, workshops, Lunch&Learns, strategic planning, executive and personal coaching, and more!)

**FOR INFO ON ALL THESE OPTIONS,
VISIT: WWW.DENASAMUELS.COM**

CPSIA information can be obtained
at www.ICGtesting.com
Printed in the USA
LVHW020035170620
658107LV00012B/582